WWW. ONYXCOFFEEBAR. COM

edwin @ f

MW00770141

The Professional Barista's Handbook

The
Professional
Barista's
Handbook

An Expert's Guide to Preparing
Espresso, Coffee, and Tea

Scott Rao

The author has taken care in preparation of this book but assumes no responsibility for errors or inaccuracies.

Photography by Alex Dubois
Email: adubois.photography@gmail.com

Book design by Rebecca S. Neimark, Twenty-Six Letters
www.twentysixletters.com

Please visit *www.theprofessionalbaristashandbook.com* for information about purchasing this book.

This book is dedicated to James,
who generously gave me my first roasting lesson
and whose coffee set the bar impossibly high.

First and foremost I would like to thank Jean Zimmer for your knowledge, guidance, and friendship. This book could not have been a reality without your encouragement and help. To Alex Dubois, I am grateful for your time, energy, and patience during our photo sessions. To Andy Schecter, Jon Lewis, James Marcotte, and Tony Dreyfuss, thank you for your insightful and expert feedback.

Contents

Introduction

When I began in the coffee business fourteen years ago, I read every book I could find about coffee. After reading all of those books, however, I felt as if I hadn't learned much about how to make great coffee. My coffee library was chock-full of colorful descriptions of brewing styles, growing regions, and recipes, with a few almost-unreadable scientific books mixed in. I would have traded in all of those books for one serious, practical book with relevant information about making great coffee in a café.

Fourteen years later, I still haven't found that book. I know many other professionals as well as some obsessive nonprofessionals would like to find that same book I've been looking for. This book is my attempt to give it to them.

—

Chapter 1

Getting Started

Equipment

There will be many opportunities throughout this book to test and practice different methods of making coffee. To get the most out of the recommended techniques it is useful to have the following equipment on hand.

- A commercial or *prosumer* (professional-quality machine designed for serious consumers) espresso machine.
- A commercial or prosumer espresso grinder.
- A tamper sized properly to form a good seal with your portafilter baskets.
- A *bottomless* or *naked portafilter*.
- Nonessential, but helpful, are a Scace Thermofilter™, a timer, a thermometer, and a gram scale.

Standards

A "shot" of espresso can mean something different from barista to barista and country to country. For the purposes of this book a shot of espresso will be broadly defined as having the following parameters.*

ESPRESSO			
BREWING RATIO	EXTRACTION PRESSURE	EXTRACTION TIME	TEMPERATURE
6.5–20 g grounds to ¾–1½ oz (21–42ml) water	8–9 bar	20–35 seconds	185°F–204°F (85°C–96°C)

These standards are not recommendations; they are simply meant to reflect common, current practices. Please refer to the appendix for a more comprehensive list of coffee, tea, espresso, and water quality standards.

Some Fundamental Terms

Extraction is the removal of mass from the grounds. Extracted substances are either *soluble* or *insoluble*.

---

* It is traditional to measure shot size volumetrically, but it is far more useful to measure shots by mass. Volumetric measurements can be misleading due to variations in crema quantity; different amounts of crema can distort one's perception of how much liquid espresso is in a shot. (See "Espresso Brewing Ratios and Standards" in Chapter 3.)

In drip coffee and espresso, "solubles" are solids and gases dissolved in the brewing liquid. Soluble solids contribute to *taste* and *brew strength* while soluble gases, or *volatile aromatics,* contribute to *aroma.*[26]

In drip coffee, "insolubles" are solids and oils held in suspension. Insoluble solids are made up primarily of large protein molecules and fragments of coffee fiber.[26] Insoluble solids and oils combine to form *brew colloids.* These contribute to aroma, *body,* and taste and alter *flavor* by trapping and later releasing soluble solids and gases[26] and by buffering *acidity.*

In espresso, insolubles are held in either a suspension or an *emulsion.* The suspended solids are primarily coffee bean cell wall fragments that contribute to body but not flavor. The emulsion is a dispersion of tiny oil droplets surrounded by liquid; these oils contribute to aroma, body, and taste and also act to decrease the perception of bitterness of an espresso* by coating the tongue.[9]

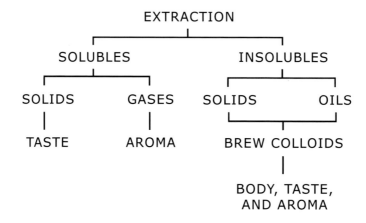

---

* An espresso tastes more bitter when made into an Americano because the addition of hot water dilutes the oil content, which prevents the oils from completely coating the tongue.

Chapter 2

Espresso

Espresso is a small, made to order, concentrated coffee consisting of liquid topped by foam, or crema. The liquid and crema are each multiphasic systems consisting of an emulsion, a suspension, and a solution.[9]

Crema is composed primarily of CO_2 and water vapor bubbles wrapped in liquid films made up of an aqueous solution of *surfactants*.[30] Crema also contains suspended coffee bean cell wall fragments, or *fines* (responsible for "tiger striping," or mottling), and emulsified oils containing aromatics.[30]

The liquid phase of an espresso consists of dissolved solids, emulsified oils, suspended fines, and an effervescence of gas bubbles.[9]

Espresso Percolation: a Primer

What follows is a general overview of espresso *percolation*. This section is not intended to be comprehensive, but rather to introduce the fundamentals.

The Basics

Espresso is produced by the percolation of pressurized hot water through a tightly packed bed of finely ground coffee. The water erodes solids and oils from the surfaces of the coffee particles as it flows through the coffee bed and deposits the solids and oils in the cup.

The flow rate of the water through the grounds is determined primarily by the amount of pressure applied by the machine, the mass of the grounds, and the fineness of the grind. Higher pressure, up to a point, increases the flow rate; beyond that pressure, flow rate decreases. A larger dose or a finer grind produce greater flow resistance and a slower flow rate.

Water always follows the path of least resistance through the coffee bed; it is the barista's job to create not only the proper amount of flow resistance, but also to form the coffee bed such that it provides uniform resistance to the water. A poorly formed coffee bed is vulnerable to the creation of a *channel,* an area of high-velocity flow through the coffee bed.

Channels are detrimental to brew strength and flavor. The large volume of water flowing through a channel dilutes the shot and causes the grounds along the channel to *overextract,** increasing bitterness. Because less water passes through the denser areas of the coffee bed, those areas *underextract,** resulting in underdeveloped flavors and lower brew strength. To minimize channeling, a barista should prepare a bed of grounds so it has a smooth and level surface, forms a tight seal with the wall of the portafilter basket, and is of uniform density.

Evidence of channeling can sometimes, but not always, be seen when using a bottomless portafilter. Channeling is indicated when extract flows more rapidly or yellows more quickly from some areas of the basket than others.

The Barista's Role

When preparing an espresso, a barista's basic goals should be to:
- Create a dose of consistent mass every shot.
- Choose the grind setting that will provide the desired flow resistance.
- Distribute the dose evenly to provide uniform resistance to the water.
- Tamp with enough pressure to eliminate void spaces within the coffee bed and to seal the surface of the bed.
- Ensure the brewing water is of the desired temperature.
- Complete all of these tasks efficiently.

The Grinder's Role

The grinder is the most important piece of equipment in an espresso bar. Grinders are usually overshadowed by more expensive, flashier espresso machines, but

---

* The terms "overextract" and "underextract" are subjective; by using them I do not mean to imply there is a universally agreed-upon ideal level of extraction for coffee, tea, or espresso. Instead, the reader should interpret overextraction as a general reference to extracting more than the intended amount, usually to the point of excessive bitterness or astringency. Underextraction is meant to indicate less extraction than intended, usually such that the resulting beverage has insufficient flavor development.

The yellow extract on the left indicates channeling.

grinder quality is arguably the single most important factor in preparing a great espresso.

A quality grinder must:
- Produce the proper particle sizes to provide adequate flow resistance.
- Create a *bimodal* or *trimodal* distribution of particle sizes. (See "Grinding for Espresso" in Chapter 2.)
- Cause minimal heating of the grounds during grinding.
- Limit the production of fines.

Fines play many important roles in espresso percolation; these will be discussed in detail in Chapter 3. For now it is important to know that the brewing water can transport and deposit fines lower in the coffee bed during percolation, a phenomenon known as *fines migration*. When fines and large insoluble protein molecules are deposited at the bottom of the coffee bed they can form a *compact layer*,[1] or densely packed solid mass. A compact layer clogs holes at the bottom of the filter basket and can result in obstruction of flow paths, uneven resistance to flow, and channeling. It is desirable to have some fines, but too many fines or too much fines migration can damage espresso quality.

The Espresso Machine's Role
The espresso machine's task is to deliver water to the grounds in a predetermined pattern of temperatures and pressures. These patterns are known as *temperature profiles* and *pressure profiles*.

A quality espresso machine should be able to produce consistent temperature and pressure profiles every shot, even under heavy use.

The Phases of Espresso Percolation

1. *Preinfusion.* Once the pump is engaged, the first phase of espresso percolation is a brief, low-pressure *preinfusion.* (Some machines skip this step and go directly to the second phase.) During preinfusion the grounds are wetted by a slow, low-pressure flow, which allows the coffee bed to reorganize itself and create a more even flow resistance.

2. *Pressure increase.* In the second phase, the pressure increases, compacting the coffee bed and increasing the flow rate. Machines without a preinfusion cycle start at this phase; such machines can make great espresso, but they are more fickle and less "forgiving" of inconsistencies on the part of the barista.

3. *Extraction.* In the third phase, extraction begins, and espresso flows from the filter basket. Extraction is primarily accomplished by the washing, or erosion, of solids from the surfaces of the ground coffee particles by the brewing water.

The eluted extract starts out relatively dark and concentrated with solids and becomes more dilute and yellow as extraction progresses. Throughout extraction, solids are removed from the coffee bed in a mostly top-down fashion; solids are preferentially removed from the upper layers of grounds. As solids are transported through the coffee bed, some settle lower in the bed, some get deposited in the compact layer, and others get extracted from the bed into the cup.

Brew Strength and Yield: Espresso
The brew strength of an espresso refers to its concentration of solids, which is between 20–60 mg/ml when using traditional Italian standards.[9] The *solids yield* of an espresso is the percentage of mass removed from the grounds during extraction; solids make up about 90% of the extracted material in an espresso.[9] Please note: when discussing espresso it is common to refer to solids concentration and solids yield, whereas when discussing drip coffee it is more appropriate to focus on solubles concentration and *solubles yield.*

Brew strength and yield have no direct relationship. For instance, using higher water temperature simultaneously increases brew strength and yield, while running extra water through a bed of grounds decreases strength and increases yield.

Grinding for Espresso

Grinding is the fracturing of coffee bean particle cells. Its purpose is to increase the amount of coffee solids exposed to the extracting liquid.

Why Espresso Requires a Very Fine Grind
Quality espresso requires an exceptionally fine grind for numerous reasons.
- It creates particles with extremely high *specific surface area,* a prerequisite for rapid washing of large quantities of solids from the particle surfaces.
- It opens more particle cells, which allows more large molecular solubles and colloidal material to be transferred to the extracting liquid.[7]

- It accelerates wetting (and *diffusion,* if it in fact occurs) by providing a shorter average path for water entering cells and solubles diffusing out of cells.[7]
- The greater specific surface area of smaller particles, along with their ability to pack together more tightly, provide the hydraulic resistance necessary for proper flow rate through the coffee bed.

Grinder Performance

I recommend you invest in the best grinder you can afford, even if it means you have to buy a cheaper espresso machine. A mediocre grinder under heavy use can damage flavor with excessive heat and can prevent even extraction by producing clumps, too many fines, or poor distribution of grounds in the basket. No espresso machine, no matter how impressive, can (yet) compensate for the problems created by poor grind quality.

The single most important feature a grinder can have is sharp burrs. This cannot be overemphasized. Sharp burrs create less strain on a grinder's motor,[7] generate less heat, produce fewer fines, and offer better particle size distribution.[11]

> Because it can be expensive to regularly purchase new burrs, I recommend you find a local machine shop or grinder manufacturer willing to resharpen dull burrs. Burrs can be resharpened several times before they need to be replaced.

How to Evaluate a Grinder

A home barista who rarely pulls more than two or three shots in an hour will probably not notice much difference in the performance of various professional-quality grinders. A home barista also has the luxury of using a time-consuming method such as the Weiss Distribution Technique to compensate for poor grinder performance. (See "Grooming" in Chapter 2.) Therefore a home barista can achieve consistently excellent results with any professional grinder of reasonable quality.

On the other hand, a barista who works in a café and frequently pulls several shots in quick succession needs to be more careful when choosing a grinder. A professional barista needs a grinder that facilitates even distribution and does not overheat the grounds when under heavy use.

The following are some important criteria for evaluating a grinder.

Minimal heating of the grounds. Some heating of the grounds is inevitable during grinding due to friction and the breaking of molecular bonds, but additional heating of the grounds due to contact with very hot grinder surfaces is undesirable. Such heating can damage coffee flavor and accelerate the loss of aromatics. It can also cause oil to bleed to particle surfaces, creating sticky clumps of grounds,* which leads to erratic percolation.[9] Clumps resist wetting and can cause large sections of the coffee bed to remain dry throughout percolation.

A well-designed grinder should have no small, enclosed spaces that trap and build up heat during heavy use. Sharper burrs, lower rotation speeds, and larger "functional" burr surfaces also mitigate the heating of the grounds during grinding. I refer to functional burr surfaces because in some grinders much of the burr surface is useless, due to the burrs being too far apart to crush the beans. The larger the functional surface, the better the heat dispersion during grinding.

Appropriate particle size distribution. Commercial espresso grinders are designed to yield bimodal (or trimodal) particle size distribution. This means the greatest frequency of particle sizes is clustered around two (or three) particular values. In such a distribution the coarser particles serve to allow proper flow, while the finer particles provide the large amount of specific surface area necessary for rapid extraction.[9] As mentioned previously, sharp burrs are necessary to optimize particle size distribution; dull burrs create a more uniform distribution of sizes.

No clumping. A grinder must be able to dispense grounds without clumps. To test your grinder, dose a couple of shots' worth of grounds onto a piece of paper and search the pile for clumps. If there are any, clean the burrs as well as the passageway between the burrs and the dosing chamber, and replace the burrs if they are worn. If the grinder still creates clumps, try the Weiss Distribution Technique. (See "Grooming" in Chapter 2.)

Clumping is caused by excessive heat generation during grinding, a grinder design that forces the grounds to squeeze through a small passageway between the

---

* I had this problem once due to using small, dull, flat burrs; upon inspecting the spent coffee pucks, I found that 20%–25% of each puck was still completely dry!

burrs and dosing chamber, or by particles with a lot of surface oils due to aging or dark roasting.

Ease of uniform distribution. Many baristi have come up with ingenious ways to improve distribution while dosing, but a good grinder should not be so dependent on a barista's skill to achieve uniform distribution.

Some dosing mechanisms facilitate uniform distribution, while others make good distribution so difficult that even the most skilled barista has difficulty achieving it. Good distribution is easiest with grinders that drop grounds vertically as opposed to diagonally into the portafilter, dispense "fluffier" grounds, or have a homogenization (blending) mechanism.

Grinding Systems: Pregrinding Versus Grinding To Order

Most commercial grinders are designed to pregrind, with the dosing chamber kept full of grounds so the barista simply needs to pull the lever one or two times to dose the required amount of grounds. This system is very fast and convenient, but it has two significant flaws: first, the weight of each dose is affected by how much ground coffee is in the dosing chamber, and that amount constantly varies. Second, the ebb and flow of business causes the grounds to spend a variable amount of time *degassing* after grinding and before *infusion*.

Degassing is the gradual release of gases, primarily CO_2 plus some volatile aromatics, produced during roasting.* Once coffee is ground, degassing dramatically accelerates.

The amount of CO_2 in the grounds is important because it influences flow rate during percolation. When hot water contacts the grounds, they vigorously release CO_2,‡ which repels the surrounding liquid and increases flow resistance, slowing the flow rate.

The pregrinding system results in inconsistent flow rates because shots are made from grounds containing variable amounts of CO_2. Inconsistent flow rates in turn cause flavor, body, and brew strength to vary.

Grinding to order is superior to pregrinding. Grinding coffee freshly for each shot preserves more aromatics and produces more consistent flow rates because shots are made from grounds with a consistent amount of CO_2. The only disadvantage of grinding to order is that it requires more time and attention to make each shot.

---

* One gram of freshly roasted Arabica coffee beans contains 2–10 mg of CO_2,[14] with most reported values in the low end of the range. In whole bean form it takes several weeks for the bulk of the CO_2 to be released; in ground form coffee degasses many times faster. One study demonstrated that 45% of the CO_2 held in freshly roasted beans was released within the first five minutes after grinding.[10] A typical espresso grind, finer than that used in the study, would release CO_2 even faster.

‡ At espresso brewing temperatures, CO_2 is more water soluble at higher pressures than at lower pressures. During espresso percolation the pressure is highest at the top of the coffee bed (typically, 9 atmospheres) and lowest at the bottom of the coffee bed (atmospheric pressure). The brewing liquid encounters progressively lower pressures as it descends the coffee bed; therefore, the preponderance of outgassing occurs in the lower coffee bed. A lot of outgassing can also occur throughout the entire coffee bed during low-pressure preinfusion.

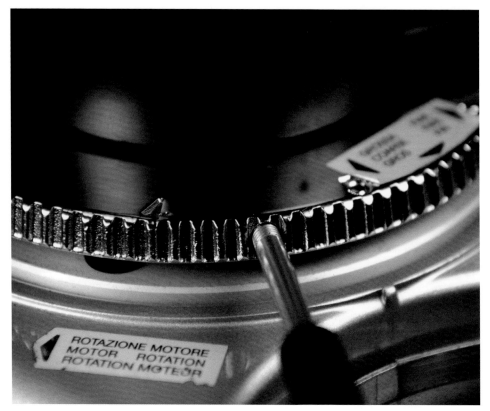

A barista should rarely adjust the grind more than one notch at a time.

Adjusting the Grind

During the normal course of business, the most important factors affecting flow rate from shot to shot are the grind and dose. Varying the dose by only 1 gram can alter the flow rate for a given shot volume by several seconds. Therefore, a barista should not adjust the grind in response to just one shot with poor flow rate if there is a chance the dose was not identical to that of previous shots. On the other hand, whenever the flow rate has trended faster or slower over the course of several shots, the barista should feel confident the grind needs adjusting.

To achieve consistent dosing a barista should:

1. Practice the same exact dosing, distribution, and *grooming* (leveling and refining of the distribution) techniques every shot.
2. Practice until he or she can consistently create a coffee bed with a variation in mass of only about 0.5 gram.
3. Periodically test his or her consistency by weighing a few doses during a busy period.

It is best to adjust the grind in small increments. If your grinder has a small tunnel between the burrs and the dosing chamber, any new grind setting should not be evaluated until the first 5 grams or so of grounds have been used or discarded. This eliminates any effect caused by "old" grounds that had been stuck in the tunnel or scattered around the dosing chamber.

Dosing and Distribution

Unlike many other coffee professionals, I consider dosing and distribution a unit, since the distribution of most of the coffee bed is determined during dosing. A barista's goal when dosing and distributing should be to provide every shot with a dose of identical mass and evenly distributed volume and density. Dose size variation leads to inconsistent flow rates, and uneven distribution causes uneven extraction.

Perhaps the single most important skill a barista can have is to be able to consistently create an evenly distributed coffee bed. Distribution starts as soon as dosing begins, so it is critical to dose with careful aim.

How to Dose
The following is one example of a dosing system.
1. Unlatch the portafilter from the espresso machine.
2. Knock out the spent puck.
3. Wipe the inside of the portafilter basket with a dry rag; moisture on the side of the basket can promote channeling around the edges of the coffee bed.
4. Ensure all of the basket holes are clear.

5. Turn on the grinder. If you have a very slow grinder, you may turn on the grinder as the first step.
5. Pull the handle repeatedly while rotating the portafilter so that the grounds fill the basket as evenly as possible. If more grounds fall into one section than another, the favored section will be more compacted, even after grooming.
7. Turn off the grinder when the proper amount has been ground.
8. Stop dosing when the desired amount is in the basket. This amount can be exactly the amount used for extraction, or it can be a little more, with the extra grounds removed during grooming. Whatever amount you choose, it is important to consistently dose the same amount every shot.

Dosing Variations

No matter what dosing method you use, it is easier to get a uniform distribution by sprinkling a small dose with each pull of the handle than by dumping large amounts of grounds with each pull. A couple of common dosing methods are efficient enough to use in a busy café.

1. *The pie piece method.* Think of the coffee bed as a pie cut into several wedge-shaped pieces. As you dose, fill each "pie piece" to the rim of the basket, rotate the portafilter and fill in the adjacent piece, rotate and fill again, and so on.
2. *The layering method.* Sprinkle small amounts around the basket while continually rotating it to form a shallow, even layer of grounds. Repeat the process to build a second layer on top of the first. Continue stacking layers until the desired dose is in the basket.

Constantly rotate the portafilter back and forth (not shown) to create layers. Always aim doses at the lowest spot on the surface of the bed.

Espresso

Grooming

After dosing and before tamping, a barista should groom the dose. Grooming involves redistributing the upper layers of the coffee bed (or, in the case of the Weiss Distribution Technique, the entire coffee bed), eliminating any extra grounds if the barista deems the dose too large, and then polishing the surface of the coffee bed before tamping.

Grooming Methods

Several common grooming methods are in use today, each with its own advantages and disadvantages.

1. *The NSEW (North South East West) Method* (not to be confused with the tamping method of the same name). The NSEW method is easy to learn and fast enough for use in a busy café.

   Using your finger or a straight-edged tool, push the mound of grounds toward the far rim of the basket (i.e., "north") without pushing the grounds over the edge. Then push the mound to the near edge ("south"), then to the right, then to the left. Finally, push any extra grounds over the edge. The surface of the bed should be smooth and level, with no divots or visible inconsistency. Using the NSEW method, it is critical that the amount of "extra" grounds in the basket prior to grooming is consistent every time. The mass of the mound before grooming heavily influences the density of the groomed bed. The end result might always look the same, but a bed that began with a larger mound of grounds before grooming will be denser after grooming.

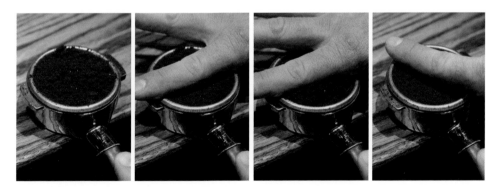

First push the grounds to the far rim of the basket (north), then back toward the handle (south), then right (east), then left (west), pushing any extra grounds over the edge before tamping.

2. *Stockfleth's Move.* Stockfleth's is perhaps the most difficult grooming technique to master but works well once you get the hang of it. Begin by slightly overdosing the basket. Hold the portafilter in front of your torso with both elbows facing outward. Put a straightened finger, or the webbing between the thumb and forefinger, gently on the grounds. Pull both elbows inward, causing the portafilter and the leveling hand to rotate in opposite directions. The mound of grounds should rotate around the center point of the

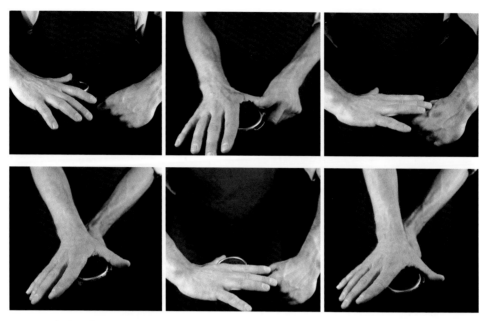

Begin with the elbows out, and pull the elbows in while rotating the mound of grounds around the center of the coffee bed. Repeat this motion two or three times.

Perform a NSEW swipe before pushing any extra grounds over the edge of the basket.

basket. Repeat the motion several times until all areas are equally filled and compacted. You may polish the surface with a quick NSEW swipe before pushing any residual grounds over the edge.

3. *The Weiss Distribution Technique (WDT).* Invented by John Weiss, the WDT is an ingenious way to compensate for clumps or uneven distribution. To execute the WDT, squeeze a funnel into the top of the portafilter basket. (John recommends using a small yogurt container with the bottom cut off.) Funnel the grinds into the basket until it is slightly overfilled. Stir the grounds well with a slender, pointed object such as a dissecting needle or straightened paper clip. Remove the funnel, groom the dose with a quick NSEW swipe or Stockfleth's Move, and tamp. Alternatively, the grounds can be dosed into a separate container and stirred before being poured into the portafilter basket. This version has the advantage of allowing the portafilter to retain more heat, since the portafilter spends less time detached from the group head.

    The WDT offers the two unique benefits of breaking up clumps and redistributing an entire dose after it is already in the basket. The disadvantage of the WDT is that it might be too time consuming for regular use in a busy café.

Ugh! Lots of clumps. Stir the grounds vigorously with a straightened paper clip to break up the clumps. The end result is fluffy, clump-free grounds.

Grooming Shallow Doses

All of the above grooming methods require starting with a mound of grounds large enough to fill the basket to the rim. Doses too small to crest the rim cannot be groomed with a level finger or tool. To groom a smaller dose, a barista has two choices: groom with a rounded tool or switch to a smaller basket.*

---

* Grooming with a convex tool results in a coffee bed with a concave surface. After tamping, such a bed is denser near its perimeter than its center. This uneven density is not ideal. However, because channels most frequently form near the perimeter of a coffee bed, such a distribution eliminates the most common source of channeling. A coffee bed groomed with a convex tool usually results in good, but imperfect, extraction patterns, and rarely forms large channels.

Use the lid of the dosing chamber or any other curved object to groom shallow doses. The greater the curvature (i.e., the smaller the object, if it is circular), the smaller the resulting dose will be.

Shallower doses can be groomed with a rounded, convex tool such as the lid of a grinder's dosing chamber. One option is to rest the object on the rim of the basket and swipe NSEW before pushing any extra grounds over the edge. Alternatively, swipe the tool until it is at the centerline of the basket, and then rotate the tool one or two revolutions in a fashion similar to Stockfleth's Move. Residual grounds can then be swiped over the edge with the rounded object.

Using a smaller basket can eliminate the need for a special grooming tool. For instance, a 15-gram dose might be shallow in one double basket but will be level with the rim in a different manufacturer's double basket. If you prefer to always groom with a level tool, it is worth having a variety of baskets on hand.

Tamping

Tamping locks in a distribution, polishes the surface of the coffee, and eliminates any large void spaces in the coffee bed. Tamping also offers a perceptive barista feedback about dose quantity, distribution, and grind.

How Hard to Tamp
Contrary to popular belief, the difference in flow resistance caused by lighter and harder tamping is minimal.[9] Once the coffee has been tamped with enough pressure to eliminate any large void spaces in the bed, additional tamping pressure will not

have much effect on extraction quality or flow rate.* Two factors account for this.

1. Some or all of the pressure generated by tamping is immediately relieved when the coffee particles are wetted.
2. The 50 lb or so of force applied by a barista when tamping firmly is dwarfed by the 500+ lb of force applied by the pump during extraction.‡

Very firm tamping does not seem to offer any benefits, but there are at least two reasons to tamp lightly: it causes less stress on the barista's wrist and shoulder, and it makes it easier for the barista to achieve a perfectly level tamp. (This is immediately clear when using a tamper and basket designed to have a very tight fit. When a barista tamps with a lot of force they will get stuck together much more frequently, indicating the tamper is not level.)

---

* One interesting reason many baristi overestimate the impact of harder tamping on flow rate is that, for a given dose and basket, a harder tamp will compact the bed more, leading to more "headspace" between the grounds and the dispersion screen. Because the entire headspace must be filled with water before the water will percolate through the grounds at full pressure, the extra headspace increases the lag time between pump activation and the appearance of extract from the portafilter. The extra lag time might lead a barista to overestimate how much the harder tamp slowed the flow rate.

‡ 9 bar pressure ≈ 130.5 psi; coffee in 58-mm basket has surface area of 4.09 sq in; 130.5 psi × 4.09 sq in = 533.7 lb.

To Tap or Not to Tap?

A recent point of contention in the tamping debate is whether to tap the side of the portafilter between tamps. The argument in favor of tapping is that it dislodges any loose grounds which had crept up the walls of the basket during the first tamp, and those grounds can then be sealed into the coffee bed with a second tamp.

It is hard to see how incorporating a few loose grounds into the coffee bed is worth the potential harm done by tapping. The tap can break the seal between the grounds and the wall of the basket, creating an easily exploitable channel around the edges of the coffee bed. In my experience a broken seal is difficult, if not impossible, to fix with a second tamp. It might be possible to tap without breaking the seal, but tapping does not seem worth the risk. The bottom line: a few loose grounds are a minor problem, if in fact they are a problem at all. (I don't think they are.) A broken seal between the grounds and the basket is a major problem.

One barista I admire taps with her wrist (an action akin to a strike with a "dead blow" hammer) in order to limit any jarring of the coffee bed. If you must tap, this seems to be a safer method than tapping with the hard handle of a tamper.

How to Tamp

Grip the tamper loosely in your hand, aligning the shaft of the tamper handle as if it were an extension of your forearm. Your wrist should be neutral, and the base of the tamper handle should sit comfortably in the hollow of your palm. This position will minimize strain on the wrist, which is critical for a barista who tamps hundreds or thousands of times per week.

Keeping the tamper level, squeeze it gently onto the grounds. That's it. There is no need for a twist or a second tamp.

When you release the tamper some loose grounds might remain on the wall of the basket or on the surface of the coffee bed. Briefly turn the portafilter upside

Hold the tamper comfortably in the hollow of your palm with the shaft of the tamper handle aligned as an extension of your forearm.

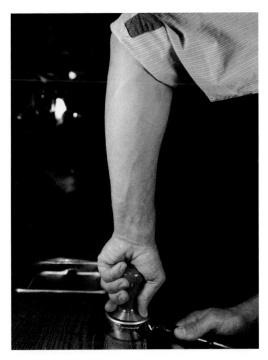

Tamp lightly with a neutral wrist to minimize strain.

The tamped coffee should have a smooth and level surface.

down if you wish to get rid of these grounds. Next, wipe the edges of the porta-filter clear of grounds. Last, latch the portafilter onto the espresso machine gently in order to avoid jolting the grounds and breaking the seal between the coffee and the basket.

Perform the above actions quickly but carefully to prevent the portafilter from losing too much heat while it is unlatched from the group head.

The Tamper

The tamper should fit snugly into the portafilter basket. If the tamper is too small it will not seal the perimeter of the coffee bed, and channeling around the edges of the bed is more likely to occur. Ideally, the tamper should fit such that if it sits the least bit crooked, it will get stuck in the basket. I have had numerous tampers machined to fit my baskets and so far have found the ideal gap between the tamper and basket to be $5/1000$ inch, i.e., a difference of $10/1000$ inch (.25 mm) in diameter. A larger gap will create a slightly higher frequency of channeling over the course of many shots.

Custom tampers can be made by a local machine shop or by a tamper manufacturer willing to make custom sizes.

Whereas most commercial tampers are machined precisely, portafilter baskets can vary tremendously in size; in a recent batch of triple baskets I bought from one supplier, the diameters varied within a range of $75/1000$ inch, or 2 mm! I have found it is easy to find double baskets of consistent size and tampers designed properly to fit those baskets; I've had less luck with triple baskets. For triples my strategy has been to order dozens of baskets, measure their diameters to within $1/1000$ inch, and return the baskets of exceptionally large or small diameter. Usually, the majority of basket diameters will be within a range of $2/1000$ inch to $3/1000$ inch; those are the ones I keep. Then I have a tamper machined to a diameter $10/1000$ inch smaller than the smallest diameter in the range.

Please note: a standard 58-mm tamper designed for single and double baskets does not fit all baskets equally and is not designed for use with triple baskets.

Water Temperature

Brewing water temperature is very important because it affects flavor, brew strength, and flow rate. The "ideal" brewing temperature is determined by numerous variables, including the coffee used, the flow rate of a shot, and, most importantly, your taste. It is fair to say almost all professionals prefer temperatures in the range of 185°F–204°F (85°C–96°C).

A few established facts exist regarding the relationship between temperature and espresso quality.
- Excessively low temperatures produce sour, underextracted espresso.
- Excessively high temperatures produce bitter, acrid, and woody flavors.[21]
- Higher temperatures result in more solids extraction and body.[21]
- Higher temperatures result in slower flow rates.[9]

Managing Brewing Temperature

Before pulling a shot, a barista should purge, or flush, water from the group head to clear coffee particles from the dispersion screen and to manipulate brewing temperature. A flush can be done with the portafilter removed or with an empty portafilter latched onto the group head.

Some flushes are done to cool the group, some to preheat the pipes feeding the

Flushing with no portafilter. Flushing can also be done with an empty porta-filter in place to preheat it.

group head, and others to purge the *heat exchanger* of overheated water. Every machine is different and requires a customized flushing routine based on the machine's design, the desired brewing temperature, the *pressurestat* setting, and other factors.

Managing Temperature on Multiple-Boiler Machines

Multiple-boiler machines have one boiler dedicated to steam production and one or more thermostatically controlled boilers dedicated to brewing water. If it is well-designed and has a *PID (proportional integral derivative) controller,* a multiple-boiler machine can produce extremely consistent brewing temperature every shot.

Such machines usually require a very short purge to produce the desired brewing temperature. The temperatures resulting from various purge amounts should be measured using a Scace Thermofilter or other bead probe thermometer.

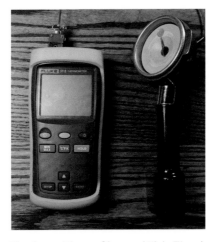

The Scace Thermofilter and Fluke™ multimeter

The temperature profile produced by a thermostatically controlled machine is considered "flat" and looks like an "L" rotated clockwise 90°. Depending on the machine, it takes between a fraction of a second and several seconds for the brewing water to reach a constant temperature.

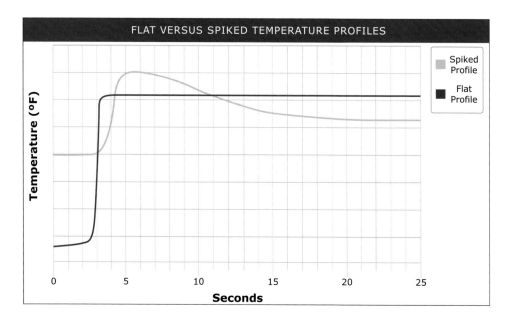

Managing Temperature on Heat-Exchange Machines

In heat-exchange machines, cold water is drawn through the heat exchanger, a small pipe within the boiler where water is flash-heated on its way to the group head. Most heat-exchange machines have a *thermosyphon loop* in which water circulates between the heat exchanger and group head. This keeps the group head hot and keeps the water cooler than it would be if it were to stagnate in the heat exchanger.

Heat-exchange machines do not dispense brewing water at a constant, or flat, temperature. Instead, as shown in the illustration, the temperature increases sharply over the first few seconds of a shot, peaks, stabilizes, and then drifts lower.*

Managing temperature on most heat-exchange machines requires three steps.

Step 1: Adjust the pressurestat. The pressurestat controls the pressure, and hence temperature, in the boiler; higher pressure leads to higher temperature. The pressure should be set low enough to limit overheating (relative to the desired temperature) of the brewing water but not so low as to compromise milk steaming pressure. If you choose to use very low boiler pressure, please note that you might need to switch to steam wand tips with smaller holes in order to maintain enough steam velocity to produce quality milk froth.

---

* Heat-exchange machines dispense water at a wide range of temperatures over the course of a shot. When I refer to a heat-exchange machine as being consistent within 1°F shot to shot, it means if you mapped the temperature profile graphs of several shots on one grid, the curves would consistently be within 1°F of each other.

Most stock pressurestats allow the boiler pressure to fluctuate by about 0.2 bar, causing temperature fluctuations of approximately 4°F (2°C). More consistent boiler temperatures can be achieved by decreasing the pressurestat's *deadband*, if it is adjustable, installing a more sensitive pressurestat, or installing a PID controller. (See the discussion of PIDs later in this chapter.)

Step 2: Adjust the thermosyphon flow restrictors, if there are any. Thermosyphon flow restrictors improve temperature consistency from shot to shot and limit the amount of cooling flush needed. The right combination of pressurestat setting and flow restrictor size in conjunction with a very short flush will allow a barista to consistently achieve any reasonable brewing temperature range with variations of less than 1°F shot to shot.

Please note: some restrictors are adjustable; others need to be replaced with a different size to alter brewing temperature.

Step 3: Temperature surfing. Heat-exchange machines without flow restrictors require much more effort on the part of the barista to achieve acceptable temperature consistency. These machines require the barista to adjust the length of the flush to the conditions of each shot, a technique known as *temperature surfing*.

To temperature surf, first flush beyond the point when the brewing water changes from sputtering (boiling) to quietly flowing, and then allow the water to run a few seconds more. The end of the sputtering indicates the heat exchanger has been fully flushed. The longer the water is allowed to flow, the cooler it will get, up to a point. As soon as the flush is halted, the water in the heat exchanger will begin to reheat. Therefore, to achieve the desired brewing temperature, a barista has to consider both the length of the flush and the time of the pause between the flush and pulling the shot.

For efficiency in a busy café, a flushing routine should be designed with minimal pause time, a technique is known as "flush and go." This consists of flushing down to the desired brewing temperature and then immediately latching on the portafilter and engaging the pump. Home baristi without concern for expediency have the luxury of experimenting with various combinations of flushes and pause times.

It is useful to accurately measure the temperatures produced by various flushing routines before settling on one. The easiest way to do this is by using a Scace Thermofilter. Other high-speed bead probe thermometers also work, but they require a fresh dose of grounds per shot to create the realistic flow resistance required for accurate temperature measurement. That can quickly make temperature measurement messy and expensive.

Spiked Versus Flat Temperature Profiles
Many coffee professionals have expended a lot of energy debating the merits of spiked versus flat temperature profiles. There is little doubt the two types of temperature profiles result in modestly different flavors in the cup. However, with all machines, extraction takes place at a wide variety of temperatures throughout the coffee bed, especially in the earlier stages of extraction. This is because the grounds absorb heat from the brewing water as it descends the coffee bed. This fact alone makes it hard to justify many baristi's slavish devotion to flat temperature profiles.

Many baristi prefer flat temperature profiles because they are easier to comprehend and reproduce. Spiked profiles are harder to replicate from shot to shot and from one machine to the next, but the bottom line is the "best" shot each profile is capable of producing is quite similar.

If you are feeling super geeky and have an extra few hundred bucks lying around, you can buy a Scace Thermofilter, a digital thermometer, and datalogging software and play with your machine's temperature profiles. To learn how to do this, refer to some informative discussions at www.home-barista.com. Go to "forums" and search for "datalogger scace fluke."

Proportional Integral Derivative Controllers
Recently PID controllers have been installed in espresso machines to precisely control brewing temperature. A PID controller works by fine-tuning the on/off cycling of the heating element.*

In a multiple-boiler machine the PID acts directly on the brewing water boiler as a precision thermostat and can consistently produce brewing temperatures within a few tenths of one degree. If you are willing to spend $6,000 to $10,000 for a multiple-boiler espresso machine, I recommend you spend an extra few hundred dollars on a PID to greatly improve temperature stability.

In a heat-exchange machine a PID controls brewing water temperature indirectly by maintaining a consistent boiler temperature, in turn making the effect of the heat exchanger more consistent. Installing a PID in a heat-exchange machine is arguably a waste of money since a reliable, precise pressurestat can achieve a comparable level of temperature consistency at much less cost. A PID does, however, provide real-time boiler temperature readings and a quick, convenient means of changing temperature settings without any guesswork.

Dispensing Temperature Versus Extraction Temperature
The temperature of the brewing water as it leaves the dispersion screen (dispensing temperature) and the actual temperatures at which the grounds extract (extraction temperature) are quite different. Many baristi obsess over dispensing temperature but don't think much about extraction temperatures. But of course extraction temperature is what determines the flavor of an espresso.

Why are they different? At the beginning of an extraction the grounds, basket, and portafilter absorb heat from the water, causing extraction temperatures to be

---

* A PID controller uses a feedback loop to control the output of the heating element based on calculations involving the "error," or the difference between the actual boiler temperature and the desired, or setpoint, boiler temperature. The PID calculates the output based on three parameters: P (proportional), I (integral), and D (derivative). The proportional calculation adjusts output based on the magnitude of the error, the integral action is based on the duration (time) of the error, and the derivative action is based on the rate of change of the error.

lower than the dispensing temperature. As an extraction progresses the coffee bed gets warmer and extraction temperatures increase, eventually approaching the dispensing temperature if enough water is run through the grounds.

The major influences on extraction temperature are:

1. Dispensing temperature. This is the dominant influence and is approximately the upper limit of extraction temperature.
2. Portafilter mass and temperature. A cold portafilter can dramatically decrease extraction temperature. To keep the portafilter hot, minimize the amount of time it is detached from the group head during dosing and tamping.
3. Grounds temperature. This factor does not vary much from shot to shot, since almost all cafés store beans at room temperature and almost all grinders dispense grounds at just above the ambient temperature.
4. Mass of the grounds (dose). The larger the mass of grounds, the more heat they will absorb from the water and the lower the initial extraction temperatures will be.
5. Mass of the water. The more water passed through a given mass of grounds, the higher the average extraction temperature will be.

Putting It All Together

Up to this point we have analyzed the various details of espresso making in isolation. I would now like to put all the parts together and describe the process of pulling a shot. Please note that this is merely one sample system; your particular equipment might necessitate a slightly different order of tasks. For instance, if you have a very slow grinder, your first action might be to turn on the grinder.

1. Unlatch the portafilter.
2. If your machine requires a long flush, start flushing now. Stop the flush when appropriate.
3. Knock out the old grounds.
4. Wipe the portafilter basket clean and dry. Ensure all basket holes are clear.
5. Turn on the grinder. (If you have a very slow grinder, you may turn on the grinder as the first step.)
6. Begin dosing. Rotate the portafilter while dosing to distribute the grounds evenly throughout the basket as it fills.
7. Turn off the grinder when you estimate the proper amount has been ground.
8. Finish dosing.
9. Groom the dose.
10. Be sure the tamper is dry and free of grounds.
11. Tamp lightly.
12. Wipe any loose grounds from the rim of the portafilter basket.
13. If your machine requires a very short flush, do it now.
14. Latch on the portafilter and engage the pump.
15. Observe the underside of the bottomless portafilter. If there is immediate channeling, consider the possible cause, address it, and return to step 1.
16. Stop the flow based on your desired shot volume or color.

17. Serve the shot immediately.
18. If the flow rate was faster or slower than desired, consider whether to adjust the grind.

What Does a Good Pour Look Like?

A barista cannot know how an espresso will taste by simply looking at the pour. However, once a barista is intimate with a particular coffee and machine, he or she can use visual cues to estimate shot quality.

The following guidelines represent a useful framework for judging shots visually. The progression of flow and color should be adjusted to your particular coffee and machine. All observations assume use of a bottomless portafilter.

If there is a preinfusion phase, once the pump is activated it should take 3–10 seconds for coffee to appear on the underside of the basket. If there is no preinfusion, the extract should appear after 2–5 seconds. Either way, we'll consider the first appearance of coffee to be time zero.

During the first 2 seconds, dark brown extract should appear from all of the holes on the underside of the basket. If coffee has appeared from some, but not all, of the holes in the first 2 seconds, it is evidence of uneven extraction.

Seconds 3–5 should see viscous brown drops of espresso fall from the basket. Any yellow at this stage indicates a channel has formed, the grind is too coarse, or the extraction temperature is inappropriate.

By 8–12 seconds, all of the drops of espresso should join into one brown/orange stream.

The color will become progressively more yellow during the rest of the flow. The full shot should be completed in 20–35 seconds, depending on the desired *espresso brewing ratio* and flavor profile.

Preinfusion

Preinfusion is a brief wetting of the grounds at low pressure prior to engaging consistent full pressure. Numerous coffee professionals, including me, have found that most forms of preinfusion, on most machines, decrease the incidence of channeling and make the espresso machine more forgiving of flawed distribution, tamping, or grind setting.

Why Preinfusion Works
The low pressure of preinfusion wets the grounds with a slower liquid flow than would be the case if the grounds were wetted at full pressure. The slower flow allows the grounds to swell, redistribute themselves, and become more adhesive before full pressure is applied. This provides two important benefits.

1. A decrease in the frequency of channeling. I've found this to be true with numerous machines; it is also consistent with the finding that "*prewetting*" (preinfusion) decreases channeling in packed percolator beds.[7]
2. A decrease in fines migration. Because fines migration is proportional to flow rate,[1] wetting with a slower flow causes more fines to get trapped by the swelling and adhesiveness of the surrounding grounds before the fines can migrate to the bottom of the coffee bed. As noted earlier in this chapter, limiting fines migration helps promote more even extraction.

I want to be clear about this because it is controversial: *Using preinfusion will not necessarily make your best shot better, but it will almost certainly result in a much higher frequency of great shots.* Even a talented, experienced barista will find that preinfusion improves his or her consistency. More importantly, in a busy café with many baristi of different skill levels, preinfusion will lead to more consistency, a higher frequency of quality shots, and less fussing with grind adjustments.

Common Preinfusion Methods

There are numerous methods of preinfusion. As long as a preinfusion method involves low-pressure infusion followed by an uninterrupted increase in pressure, it is probably beneficial to use. The following are some of the most commonly used methods:

Manual preinfusion. The barista begins infusion at low pressure and controls when to engage full pressure. This is a feature of lever machines and some semi-automatic machines.

Manual preinfusion requires experimentation to determine the best combination of preinfusion time and pressure. A good starting point is to set the line pressure feeding the espresso machine to 3.5–4.5 bar (51–65 psi), and to sample the results produced by preinfusion times ranging from 3–10 seconds.

How the triple ristretto was born (a fictional story):

A long time ago, in a little town in the hills near Trieste, many old Italian men gathered every morning at Hilly Caffe to argue and gesticulate wildly while drinking beautiful, small cappuccini. This went on for many decades, and the men were happy because they thought the cappuccini at Hilly Caffe had a perfect balance of milk and espresso flavor. Then one day an American businessman named "The Milk Man" visited Hilly Caffe. The locals eyed the stranger warily and sensed he did not approve of their coffee ritual, for he always ordered an espresso and an enormous pitcher of steamed milk and then combined it all in an obscenely large paper cup.

Upon returning home, The Milk Man opened a chain of cafés in order to share his charming Italian experience with Americans. These cafés had little ambience, no gesticulating Italian men, and no 6-oz cappuccini, however what his cafés did have was very large paper cups filled with a little bit of espresso and a whole lot of steamed milk. Luckily for the businessman, "bigger is better" is as true in America as "the Pope is Catholic" is in Italy.

While this man was busy making billions of dollars serving lots of hot milk with a little bit of espresso another café owner was busy obsessing over making tiny, dark espresso shots and café lattes with pretty pictures on them. One day this second man, named "The Temperature Guy," wrote a book about dark espresso shots and pretty lattes. The book was called *Obsessing Over Temperature Stability*. It sold many copies. It is not known whether The Milk Man ever read the book.

Before the book was written, lots of baristi in little cafés across America made big café lattes in an attempt to get rich like The Milk Man. But they couldn't compete with The Milk Man because they didn't have his genius for marketing and real estate. Luckily, The Temperature Guy's book came along with the answer to how to make a better latte than The Milk Man's: the double ristretto.

After reading The Temperature Guy's book, baristi began using double baskets to make small, dark shots, and they began grinding each shot to order. Grinding each shot individually required baristi to use *finger-strike dosing*, as instructed by The Temperature Guy. Finger-strike dosing involves dosing the grounds up to, or above, the rim of the basket, and then leveling the dose with a finger. Baristi who used finger-strike dosing ended up, perhaps inadvertently, using larger doses than the baskets were designed for.[6]

Progressive preinfusion. Infusion begins at low pressure while water fills a spring-loaded preinfusion chamber attached to the group head. Once water has filled the empty spaces in the group head and preinfusion chamber, the spring is extended, allowing the pressure applied to the coffee bed to increase gradually.

Flow restriction. A small restrictor, or *gicleur,* decreases the flow of water to the group head. This causes a lag between the initial wetting and the application of full pressure. Some do not consider this genuine preinfusion, but flow restriction can have a preinfusion-like effect. Installing a small gicleur is a smart alternative for machines not designed to offer low-pressure preinfusion. Gicleurs of different sizes are available through many espresso parts suppliers.

Electronic preinfusion. Pump pressure is cycled on and off either once or several times during the first couple of seconds of infusion. This type of preinfusion does not adequately wet the coffee bed and seems to offer no clear benefits. I do not recommend its use.

Other Considerations
When adding a preinfusion cycle, it is necessary to adjust the grind setting finer to maintain a given flow rate. Factors such as the group head design, the spray head pattern, and the amount of space between the dispersion screen and the top of the

Even after adopting The Temperature Guy's methods, many quality-conscious American baristi were still not satisfied with the strength of the coffee flavor in their café lattes. To make their lattes stronger they were faced with a dilemma: either use two portafilters for each big latte, or use one portafilter with an *even bigger* dose of grounds. Using two portafilters for one beverage was too time consuming, so these baristi adopted the triple ristretto.

The use of such large doses had many ripple effects on espresso quality and caused baristi to make adjustments. Larger doses absorb more heat from the brewing water, so baristi began using higher brewing temperatures. Larger doses offered more hydraulic resistance, so coarser grinds were used to maintain the traditional (some would say dogmatic) 25-second extraction time. Perhaps most importantly, because baristi increased dose sizes without increasing shot sizes, they increased espresso brewing ratios.

The espresso brewing ratio is the ratio of the mass of a dry dose of grounds to the mass of a shot produced by the grounds. Higher espresso brewing ratios produce shots with lower solids yields; such shots are typically brighter and more acidic, and often sour or sharp. Shots made with lower espresso brewing ratios tend to have higher solids yields, mellower flavor profiles, and more bittersweet and caramel tones.

Recently, a very smart man named Jim wrote a paper[6] in which he discussed the effects of very large doses on solubles yield and flavor profile.* Immediately all of the geekiest American baristi read Jim's paper, and many scratched their heads, wondering what to do with the new information. Ironically, many of them rediscovered the virtues of making espresso the way the baristi always have at Hilly Caffe.

Meanwhile, the men at Hilly Caffe are still enjoying their small, caramel-sweet espressi and cappuccini. Once in a while a traveling American barista enters Hilly Caffe, and all the men stop their arguing and gesticulating to listen to what the American orders. And when the American orders caffe *normale,* they nod and smile and return to their arguments.

---

* The paper referred to solubles yield, not solids yield. Jim has since revised some of his findings, but the bulk of the paper is still a valuable resource for baristi.

coffee bed all affect the results produced by preinfusion. As with so many of the parameters of espresso making, experimentation and blind tasting are required to get the most out of any machine and coffee.

Espresso-Making Techniques in Italy Versus America

In the past two decades, non-Italian baristi have developed new espresso-making techniques, and many espresso cultures have drifted from the traditional Italian methods. In this section I will focus on the differences between Italian and American dosing and temperature standards.

Dosing Standards
In Italy the typical dose is approximately 6.5–7 grams per single (1-oz or 30-ml) shot and 13–14 grams per double (2-oz or 60-ml) shot. Historically, these parameters, in conjunction with pregrinding and standard single and double baskets have produced an accepted range of espresso brewing ratios and brew strengths.

Recently many American baristi have taken to using larger doses, often greater than 20 grams. Among the more progressive baristi, the typical dose for a single shot has evolved from a 7-gram Italian-style dose to a 14-gram double *ristretto,* to an overdosed (more than 14 grams) double ristretto, and, finally, to a triple ristretto. These shots are not ristretto in the traditional sense (i.e., very short shots made from single doses) but are shots of standard volume (1–1½ oz) made from larger (and larger) doses. These new dosing standards are not universal, but they are relevant because they are used in many of the most admired cafés. This evolution of dose sizes was an adaptation to two developments: larger American drink sizes and the popularity of grinding to order.

Temperature Differences Between Italy and America
I've often wondered why so many Italian baristi use dispensing temperatures in the 185°F–195°F (85°C–91°C) range, while many American baristi, especially those considered very progressive, use 198°F–204°F (92°C–96°C). I think one part of the answer is most Italian baristi use 7-gram doses to yield 1-oz shots, whereas many Americans use 18–21 grams to yield 1-oz shots. Despite the differences in dispensing water temperatures, both systems result in similar average extraction temperatures.

Why is that? Because the larger dose used by Americans absorbs more heat from the brewing water.

To illustrate, here is an interesting thought experiment: If you were to put 7 grams of 80°F (27°C) grounds and 30 grams of 190.5°F (88°C) water (potential inputs of a typical 1-oz Italian "Hilly Caffe" shot) in a preheated container, the mixture's temperature would be 181.1°F (82.8°C). If you then put 21 grams of 80°F (26.7°C) grounds in an identical container with 38 grams of 203.5°F (95.3°C) water (potential inputs of a typical 1-oz American "The Temperature Guy" shot), that mixture would also measure at 181.1°F (82.8°C). It is assumed each gram of grounds absorbs 1 gram of water.

The data used in the thought experiment is depicted more clearly in the following chart:

DRY COFFEE/HOT WATER MIXTURE AT EQUILIBRIUM TEMPERATURE		HILLY CAFFE	TEMPERATURE GUY
Water mass (excluding waste)	(g)	30	38
Water temperature	(°F)	190.5	203.5
Dry coffee mass	(g)	7	21
Dry coffee temperature	(°F)	80	80
Dry coffee specific heat		0.4	0.4
Approx espresso mass	(g)	23	17
Approx vol/mass ratio		0.04	0.06
Approx gross volume	(oz)	0.9	1.0
Equilibrium temperature	(°F)	181.1	181.1

How these calculations were made:
Hilly Caffe: $181.1 = (30 \times 190.5 + (7 \times 80 \times 0.4)) \div (30 + (7 \times 0.4))$
Temperature Guy: $181.1 = (38 \times 203.5 + (21 \times 80 \times 0.4) \div (38 + (21 \times 0.4))$

A sincere thank you to Andy Schecter for teaching me about *specific heat* and reworking these numbers to make them accurate.

Systems for Making Great Straight Shots and Great Milk Drinks
The best shot for straight espresso is not the same as the best shot for a 12-oz café latte. A straight espresso should have moderate brew strength and optimize the potential flavor profile of the blend used. A shot with too little brew strength will lack body because brew strength and body are highly correlated; too much brew strength will interfere with an espresso drinker's ability to perceive subtler flavors.

The ideal shot for a 12-oz latte needs to have enough mass and brew strength to balance the volume of the milk. The flavor profile of such a shot is important, but not nearly as important as the flavor profile of a straight shot because in a latte much of the espresso's subtler flavors are blunted by the milk.

To accommodate the needs of both espresso drinkers and latte drinkers, most quality cafés in the US simply use one large dose size for all shots. This can result in reasonably good straight shots and lattes, but it is expensive and wasteful and does not simultaneously optimize shots for lattes and straight espresso.

I recommend two systems that cafés can use to tailor shots to their intended purposes.

Use two separate grinders: One way to pull two distinctly different types of espresso shots is to use two different coffees and grinders. Additionally, depending on the espresso machine, one group head can be dedicated to straight shots, with its temperature tailored to the coffee being used.

Use different basket sizes and customized dosing and grooming methods: If a barista uses the traditional Italian dosing standards of 7 grams for a single and 14 grams for a double, the resulting shots will all have roughly the same brew strength, flavor, and flow rate. However, if a barista uses finger-strike dosing with single and double baskets, the dose in the double basket will be less than twice the size of the dose in the single basket.* This will result in different flow rates (faster in the double), brew strengths, and flavor profiles.

An alternative system is to use two or three different basket sizes with customized dosing and grooming systems for each. For instance, at home I have one grinder, one single basket, and one double basket. I like to use the single basket to make a mellow, sweet espresso normale with moderate brew strength and the double basket to make a double ristretto with more body and brew strength for a cappuccino. If I groom the double basket with a level tool and groom the single basket with the round lid of my grinder's dosing chamber, both baskets will yield 1-oz shots of similar mass and flow rate. Moreover, each shot will be of the desired espresso brewing ratio, flavor, and brew strength for its intended purpose.

---

* It will be roughly 1.5 times as much; the exact ratio depends on the coffee, dosing method, and the type of basket used. The examples described assume all single shots have identical mass and all double shots have twice the mass of the single shots.

Pressure Interruptions During Espresso Brewing

While a shot is being pulled, several events can temporarily decrease pressure. (These concerns do not apply to lever machines.)

1. Purging or flushing another group
2. Pulling a shot on another group
3. Engagement of the automatic boiler fill valve
4. Other machines filling, decreasing line pressure to the espresso machine

Such variations in pressure can promote channeling in the original shot and should be avoided whenever possible, using a few simple strategies.

1. Do not purge a group until all shots on other groups have been completed.
2. To pull two shots, purge both groups and prepare both portafilters before starting both shots simultaneously.*
3. Rewire your machine to prevent opening of the boiler fill valve while the pump is engaged.
4. If other machines (brewer, dishwasher, etc.) are competing with the espresso machine for water pressure, the espresso machine can be protected with the following setup. In order, from the upstream source to downstream, install water treatment, pressure bladder tank, pressure restrictor, and espresso machine. The water treatment is first because the pressure output of most systems fluctuates. The pressure fluctuations are then absorbed by the bladder, a balloon that exerts a high, constant downstream pressure regardless of the pressure upstream of it (within reason). The high-pressure output from the bladder is then decreased by the restrictor to the desired inlet pressure of the espresso machine. The bladder and restrictor combination should cost about $200.

---

* Busy baristi will find strategies 1 and 2 impossible to consistently implement without slowing service too much. That said, all baristi should make use of these strategies as often as is practical.

Chapter 3

The Science and Theory of Percolation and Extraction

I researched and wrote this chapter to teach baristi about the dynamics of espresso percolation. Some will find this section fascinating and satisfying; others will find it mind numbing. I believe it is worth the effort to read and understand, especially because it will provide knowledge that is necessary to diagnose many percolation and extraction problems.

Percolation Dynamics

The dynamics of espresso percolation are very complicated and not completely understood, but some useful models have been developed to describe what is known of the process. These models will be easier to visualize if we first discuss and observe the more familiar interaction of grounds, gases, and water in a filter during drip coffee brewing. This can be done with a manual pourover or any drip brewer that allows the grounds to be viewed during brewing.

The Dynamics of Percolation and Extraction: Drip Coffee

Phase 1: wetting Water is showered onto the coffee bed, wetting the grounds and causing them to rapidly release CO_2. The emitted CO_2 repels the water and causes *turbulence,* inhibiting both the wetting of the grounds and the flow of liquid through the coffee bed. The turbulence is evidenced by the layer of foam covering the spent grounds after brewing.

Water always follows the path(s) of least resistance through the grounds and therefore flows down the coffee bed somewhat erratically. The water both removes solids from the grounds and gets absorbed by the grounds, causing the unabsorbed liquid to become progressively more concentrated as it descends the coffee bed. The grounds swell as they absorb liquid.

Phase 2: extraction The coffee exiting the bottom of the filter is initially viscous and concentrated. As extraction proceeds, the exiting liquid becomes more dilute because there is less readily extractable material available in the coffee bed.

Extraction occurs in two phases. In the first phase, solids are washed off the surfaces of the grounds. In the second phase, solids are transferred from the inner coffee particles to the water by inner-particle diffusion,[8] the movement from an area of higher concentration to an area of lower concentration.

Diffusion occurs in a series of steps. First, water contacts the coffee particles and drives out gases. Second, water enters the pores of the particles, the particles swell, and solids within the particles dissolve. Third, the dissolved solids diffuse to the particle surfaces and then into the surrounding solution.[8]

During brewing, water is continually added to the top of the system, diluting the turbulent pool of liquid, grounds, and gases. This dilute liquid near the top of the coffee bed effects rapid diffusion from the upper layers of grounds due to a steep *concentration gradient* (the difference between the concentration of coffee solids within the grounds and within the surrounding liquid). Extraction is slower in the lower coffee bed because the liquid there is more concentrated with solids, reducing the concentration gradient. The result is uneven extraction, with more solids removed from the upper than the lower coffee bed.*

The Dynamics of Percolation and Extraction: Espresso

The dynamics of espresso and drip percolation are similar, although espresso extraction is accomplished primarily by washing, with little or no role played by diffusion. The models developed to describe espresso percolation are not comprehensive, but they have shown validity by successfully predicting the results of real-world experiments.[1,2,3,4,5] The following is derived from a combination of published research and the current knowledge base of the specialty coffee industry.

Phase 1: wetting In the first phase, water fills the headspace of the extraction chamber, driving out gases[2] and wetting the grounds. The grounds absorb water, while simultaneously the water picks up solids from the grounds. The absorption of water causes the particles to swell[9] and the coffee bed to decrease in porosity.[2]

---

* Extraction from the upper and lower coffee bed can be made more equal by using a cone-shaped, rather than cylindrical, basket. (See the discussion of basket shape later in this chapter.)

As the water flows through the bed it erodes solids from the grounds, transports the solids, and deposits some of them lower in the bed.[5] This causes the solids content of the lower coffee bed to *increase** during the wetting phase.[5,6]

The coffee bed is exceptionally vulnerable to channeling during the wetting phase. The lack of cohesion of the dry particles, reorganization of the coffee bed due to particle migration and swelling, high rates of solids removal, and, in some machines, an abrupt increase in pressure during this phase all increase the likelihood of channels forming.

By the end of the wetting phase the coffee bed has been radically transformed: it has lost porosity, swelled, and absorbed heat from the brewing water, gases have been driven out, solids have been transferred from the upper to the lower coffee bed, preferential paths have been created, and channels might have formed.

Phase 2: pressure increase A pressure gradient causes the water to flow from the area of high pressure above the coffee bed to the area of low pressure at the outlet of the filter basket. According to Darcy's Law of fluid dynamics, as the applied pressure increases, the flow of water through the coffee bed will increase. However, empirical evidence in published research[1] apparently contradicts Darcy's Law in two ways. In this study:

1. As pressure increased during extraction, flow rate initially increased, then peaked and decreased, leveling off asymptotically to a nearly constant rate.
2. In a sample of several shots pulled with various applied pressures, shots pulled with higher pressure had higher flow rates, but only up to a certain pressure. Beyond that pressure the average flow rate either remained constant or decreased. What this means in plain English is, if you were to increase your espresso machine's pump pressure from 9 bar to 12 bar, the flow rate of your shots might decrease.

Several possible reasons explain why the flow rate might decrease during the phase of increasing pressure. First, particle swelling during this phase due to the wetting of any remaining dry coffee decreases the porosity of the bed and causes an increase in hydraulic resistance. Second, the increase in pressure causes the coffee bed to compact,[13] increasing hydraulic resistance. Finally, the increased pressure "favors displacement of coffee bed particles (i.e., fines migration) and a gradual compaction of the coffee bed as a reaction."[2]

Phase 3: extraction Researchers offer conflicting opinions regarding the relative contributions of washing and diffusion to extraction in different forms of brewing. One researcher who compiled data concluded the dominant mechanism of extraction was the washing of solids from the outer surfaces of coffee particles.[27] Another analyzed the same data and concluded that 85%–90% of extraction in the first minute (and presumably 100% thereafter) was due to inner-particle diffusion.[28] If this second researcher is correct, diffusion could play a role in espresso extraction.

---

* It is not known how much of the reported increase is due to deposited solids and how much is attributable to solids being transferred through the lower bed in the extracting liquid when the process was interrupted and measurements were taken.

THE DYNAMICS OF ESPRESSO PERCOLATION AND EXTRACTION

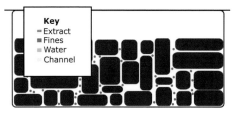

DRY
T=-10 seconds

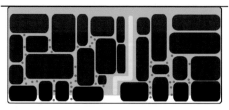

LOW PRESSURE WETTING
T=-1 second

FULL PRESSURE & FIRST EXTRACT
T=0 seconds

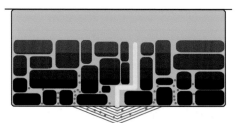

BEGINNING OF EXTRACTION
T=5 seconds

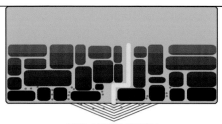

MID-EXTRACTION
T=15 seconds

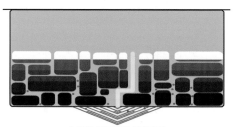

LATE EXTRACTION
T=25 seconds

The color of the grounds (represented by the stacked rectangles) in the first frame is deep red, indicating they are concentrated with coffee solids. The lighter reds in later frames represent lower solids concentrations.

T = -10 seconds: *The dry grounds just before the pump is engaged.* The grounds are packed with solids, and fines are scattered throughout the coffee bed.

T = -1 second: *The coffee bed near the end of preinfusion.* The water has percolated through almost all of the coffee bed but extraction has not yet begun. The grounds have absorbed water, swelling the coffee bed. A channel, represented by the yellow line, has formed through the middle of the coffee bed. The upper layers of the coffee bed have lost solids, while the lower coffee bed has gained solids. Fines have begun to migrate down the coffee bed.

T = 0 seconds: *The first extract appears.* The first extract appears at the outlet of the channel. Fines and solids have concentrated in the lower layers of the coffee bed. The coffee bed contracts as pressure increases.

T = 5 seconds: *Early extraction.* Solids and fines are rapidly removed from the coffee bed. The coffee bed is further compressed as full pump pressure is applied.

T = 15 seconds: *Mid-extraction.* The coffee bed shrinks as it loses mass. The upper layers of the bed are almost depleted of extractable solids. The bulk of fines and solids are concentrated in the lowest layers of the bed.

T = 25 seconds: *Final moments of extraction:* The upper layers of the bed are completely empty of extractable solids. The coffee bed has lost about 20% of its original dry mass.

The Science and Theory of Percolation and Extraction

According to the research done with large percolator columns, diffusion does not occur until coffee particles are:

1. "Satisfied with bound water." Coffee particles can hold up to about 15% of their dry weight as bound water.[16]
2. Saturated with free extracting liquid.[7]
3. Free of gases.[7]

The typical espresso extraction time is probably too short for all three preconditions of diffusion to be met. Therefore, it is likely that espresso extraction is accomplished entirely by the washing of solids from the outer surfaces of coffee particles, as well as by the emulsification* of oils.[9] Diffusion plays little, if any role.

Flow Progression
The initial extract from the flow of a well-prepared shot should be viscous and dark.‡ As the flow progresses the extract becomes more dilute and the color gradually lightens, eventually turning yellow. Cutting off the flow when it yellows, or

---

* The emulsification of oils seems to be enabled by the pressure of espresso brewing. It is arguable that the emulsion is the aspect of an espresso most responsible for differentiating it from a very concentrated cup of coffee.

‡ The color of the extract is believed to be darker when it has a higher concentration of caramelized solids or a lower concentration of CO_2, though there may be other factors that influence color.

"blondes," limits dilution of brew strength but has less effect on flavor than is commonly believed, because the extract has a very low concentration of flavoring material in the later stages of extraction.

Solids removal from the upper layers of the coffee bed is rapid during wetting and early extraction.[5] This is due to the presence of high temperatures, the relative ease of particle migration during the wetting phase, and the presence of a steep concentration gradient.

In the lower layers solids content initially increases during wetting and then stabilizes during early extraction[5] as the lower coffee bed loses smaller, fast-dissolving solids and simultaneously gains deposited fines. The net result is that the upper layers of the coffee bed contribute a much greater percentage of solids to the cup than do the lower layers.[5,6]

Fines

Migration of fines, or ultra-fine cell wall fragments, is the "x factor" of espresso percolation. Though I am not aware of any direct measurement quantifying fines migration, there is quite a bit of indirect evidence of its existence in published research[1,6,7,9] and in the predictive ability of mathematical models* that are based on the assumption that fines migrate and form a compact layer at the bottom of the coffee bed.[1,4,5]

Formation of a significant compact layer can disrupt even percolation by obstructing holes on the bottom of the filter basket. Formation of a compact layer can harm espresso quality by causing several problems.

1. An unintended reduction in flow rate. Any barista who has experienced a decrease in flow rate during extraction was probably witnessing the result of increased hydraulic resistance caused by growth of the compact layer.
2. Uneven extraction patterns and channeling.
3. Reduction in body, if too many fines settle in the layer instead of contributing solids (both soluble and insoluble) to the cup.

The Effects of Fines on Espresso Quality
Beyond the formation of a compact layer, fines have positive and negative effects on espresso quality. To gain insight into the effects of fines, I used a 90-micron sieve to remove a large quantity, perhaps the majority, of fines from the grounds before dosing.‡ The first apparent effect of removing the fines was a faster flow rate,

---

* Some of the mathematical models referred to have been used to create espresso percolation simulations able to accommodate numerous input variables. Real-world experiments have validated the predictions of these models for such values as percentage of a coffee bed wetted during preinfusion, quantities of solids remaining in different layers of a coffee bed after extraction, and percolation flow rates.

‡ I did not quantify the proportion of fines I removed; I simply shook the sieve for about a minute, at which point no more fines were passing through the sieve.

which indicated that fines provide flow resistance. After adjusting the grind finer to rebalance the flow rate, I pulled several shots with the sieved grounds. Compared to "normal" shots from the same beans, the mostly fines-free shots had less body and less bitterness.

Because the presence of fines contributes positively (more body) and negatively (more bitterness) to espresso, the best espresso should result from finding the ideal proportion of fines for a given dose size and by limiting the migration of those fines to prevent formation of a compact layer. There is no practical way to measure fines production or migration, however, there are methods of decreasing fines production and migration.

Limiting Fines Production
Production of fines is inevitable during grinding due to the brittleness of roasted beans. For a given grind setting, there are four ways to reduce the quantity of fines produced: use sharper burrs,[11] use a lighter roast,[7] use slower grinding speeds,[7] or use beans with higher moisture content.[7]

Limiting Fines Migration
A barista can monitor fines migration indirectly in two ways: by observing the uniformity of extract flow and color with a bottomless portafilter and by inspecting the filter basket holes after knocking out spent grounds. (Color should not vary too much from area to area, and the filter basket holes should be clear.) Based on these observations a barista can decide whether fines migration is excessive.

The most effective way to reduce fines migration is by using low-pressure preinfusion. Fines migration is also decreased by use of a finer grind. A finer grind shrinks migration pathways by decreasing the space between grounds and allowing more compaction of the coffee bed.[7] Of course, simply making the grind finer will result in a slower flow rate, but a finer grind used in conjunction with a smaller dose or a wider basket can balance the flow rate.

Basket Shape and Extraction

A standard single basket is shaped like a truncated cone, while a standard double basket is cylindrical, or nearly so. Does basket shape affect extraction quality? The answer is a qualified yes.

Earlier in this chapter it was noted that the upper layers of the coffee bed yield more solids than do the lower layers during extraction.[5,6] Such uneven extraction is detrimental to flavor and brew strength: the upper layers overextract, yielding bitterness and astringency, and the lower layers underextract, resulting in less sweetness, less brew strength, and perhaps some underdeveloped flavors.

The use of cylindrical baskets exacerbates this uneven extraction, whereas using truncated-cone baskets can balance some or all of it. To explain, consider a hypothetical set of well-prepared extractions, one in a cylindrical basket, and the other in a truncated-cone basket. For the moment let's assume fines do not migrate and

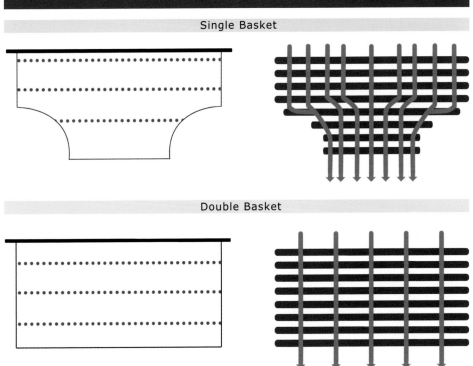

Single Basket

Double Basket

no significant channels form in either extraction. Imagine you can see inside the coffee beds during the extractions. In your mind's eye cut each bed into a series of thin horizontal layers, or cross sections. (Visualize the layers as a stack of discs.)

In a cylindrical double basket the volume of liquid flowing through each layer is equal. (Let's ignore the effect of water absorption for the moment.*) Also, the area of each layer is identical. Therefore the volume of liquid flow per unit area is the same in all layers.

In a truncated-cone basket the volume of liquid flowing through each layer is also equal. However, the upper layers have larger areas, and the liquid encounters layers of less and less area as it descends the coffee bed. Therefore, during extraction the volume of liquid flow per unit area increases as the liquid descends. (Think of it as a road merging from two lanes into one; the same volume of cars flows down the road before and after the merge, but the volume per lane doubles after the merge.)

In a single basket, the greater flow per unit area in the lower layers results in higher extraction yield from those layers. Therefore, in these hypothetical extractions, the shape of the single basket provides a more uniform extraction.

---

* In real life, grounds absorb water. This makes calculating the flow through each layer complicated, but it doesn't change the fact that there is greater liquid flow, and hence extraction, per unit area in the lower layers of a truncated-cone basket than in the lower layers of a cylindrical basket.

The same dynamic applies to drip coffee baskets; using a cone-shaped basket will result in more uniform extraction from the coffee bed. Consumer drip brewers with cone-shaped baskets are readily available. However, I know of no commercial drip brewers that come with cone-shaped baskets. With commercial machines that offer a variety of compatible baskets, it is best to use the most tapered basket available.

Espresso Brewing Ratios and Standards

What is a ristretto? A normale? A *lungo?*

Whereas there is a semblance of standards in Italy, in the rest of the world espresso is made with a great variety of doses and shot sizes. Consequently, those three terms have come to mean very different things to different baristi.

It is understood that at a given café a normale is a standard shot, a ristretto is made with the same dose but less water, and a lungo is made with the same dose but more water. Therefore the three terms refer loosely to espresso brewing ratios.*

Traditionally, baristi have measured shot size by volume, with 1 oz, or 30 ml, being the standard Italian normale. This presents a complication: because the crema volume of different shots can vary tremendously, the amount of liquid espresso in two shots of the same volume can also vary quite a bit. Any barista who has watched several shots rest for a few minutes can attest to the fact that the amount of liquid remaining after the crema has dissipated can be very inconsistent.

Crema volume is increased by using fresher beans, grinding immediately before pulling a shot, adding robusta, using a bottomless portafilter, and other factors.

The proper way to compare espresso brewing ratios and shot "sizes" is to weigh doses and shots. During service in a café it is impractical to weigh shots as they extract; I do not propose baristi weigh all their shots, but I think they should weigh shots intermittently to improve consistency. Weighing shots also allows baristi to communicate more effectively when discussing shot doses, sizes, and espresso brewing ratios.

The concept of espresso brewing ratios based on shot mass instead of volume is the brainchild of my friend Andy Schecter, a brilliant amateur coffee scientist from Rochester, New York.‡

It is interesting to note that a barista who pulls shots using a machine's pro-grammable volumetric buttons will achieve a far more consistent espresso brewing ratio than a barista stopping shots by sight. Shots produced with the programmable buttons can vary by volume due to differences in crema quantity, but they will in fact be of reasonably consistent mass.

---

* The term *brewing ratio* is traditionally used in reference to drip coffee brewing; it is the ratio of dry grounds to brewing water used to make a coffee. In espresso making it is difficult to measure the quantity of water used due to the high and variable proportion of the brewing water absorbed by the grounds. Therefore it is practical, if a bit of a misnomer, to define espresso brewing ratio as the ratio of the mass dry grounds to the mass of the shot.

‡ Andy's discussion of these ideas, as well as the original publication of the following chart, appear at: http://www.home-barista.com/forums/brewing-ratios-for-espresso-beverages-t2402.html.

How should baristi use this information about shot mass and espresso brewing ratios? First, I think baristi should weigh a few shots per day to help maintain consistency. Second, when discussing extractions, roasters and seasoned baristi should include information about shot mass, just as they do about dose size and water temperatures. Third, baristi should experiment with using the programmable volumetric buttons, with the caveat that shots still need to be monitored for flow rate and channeling.

BREWING RATIOS FOR ESPRESSO COFFEE		DRY COFFEE (g)			BEVERAGE (g)			BREWING RATIO (DRY/LIQUID)			GROSS VOLUME INCL. CREMA (oz)	
		LOW	MED	HIGH	SMALL	MED	LARGE	LOW	HIGH	TYPICAL	LOW*	HIGH**
RISTRETTO	SINGLE	6	7	8	4	7	13				0.3	0.6
	DOUBLE	12	16	18	9	16	30	60%	140%	100%	0.7	1.3
	TRIPLE	19	21	23	14	21	38				0.9	1.7
REGULAR ESPRESSO NORMALE	SINGLE	6	7	8	10	14	20				0.6	1.1
	DOUBLE	12	16	18	20	32	45	40%	60%	50%	1.3	2.6
	TRIPLE	19	21	24	32	42	60				1.9	3.4
LUNGO	SINGLE	6	7	8	15	21	30				0.8	1.5
	DOUBLE	12	16	18	30	48	67	27%	40%	33%	1.9	3.3
	TRIPLE	19	21	24	48	63	89				2.5	4.4
CAFE CREMA	SINGLE	6	7	8	38	50	67				1.8	3.0
	DOUBLE	12	16	18	75	114	150	12%	16%	14%	4.0	6.9
	TRIPLE	19	21	24	119	150	200				5.3	9.0
DRIP COFFEE	SCAA STANDARD		55			1000		5%	6%	5.5%		

*OLDER BEANS; SPOUTED PF; 100% ARABICA; LEVER MACHINE   **FRESH BEANS; NAKED PF; USE OF ROBUSTA; PUMP @ 9 BAR

In this chart Andy Schecter defines ristretto, normale, and lungo using espresso brewing ratios. Not all baristi will agree with Andy's definitions, but his proposed standards reflect common practices in Italy, and his definitions happen to be eloquently simple and easy to remember. To translate, Andy's typical ristretto is defined as having mass equal to the dry grounds used to make it. The weight of a typical normale, or "regular espresso," is twice the weight of the dry grounds used, and a typical lungo is three times the weight of the dry grounds used. *Café crema* is simply a very long pull of espresso.

Chapter 4
Milk

Milk Steaming

Milk is the primary ingredient by volume in most espresso beverages. As such, its preparation deserves the same care and attention given to espresso extraction.

Much like choosing a coffee roaster, choosing a milk supplier should be based on quality and blind taste testing. Milk should be sampled both cold and frothed and with and without espresso.

Baristi should be aware that the quality of milk from any supplier fluctuates throughout the year due to changes in the weather and the content of the dairy cows' diets. Some years I have had to switch suppliers seasonally, since one supplier's milk was better in the winter and another supplier's was better in the summer.

Milk Steaming Goals

The following should be the basic goals of any barista when steaming milk.

- Pour only as much milk as you will need for the current drink(s).
- Create a tight micro-bubble structure when aerating milk; the surface should be glassy and have no visible bubbles.
- Heat the milk to a final temperature of 150°F–160°F (66°C–71°C).
- Plan ahead so milk steaming and espresso extraction are completed at about the same time.
- Serve drinks before they separate!

Milk Separation

The *mouthfeel* of a cappuccino or café latte before the milk has separated is far superior to the mouthfeel of the same drink a minute or two later. The sin of allowing a drink to sit and separate before it is consumed is analogous to allowing a shot of espresso to age before it has been drunk. In each case the beverage is unstable and its quality declines if it is not consumed in a timely manner. While there is no guarantee a customer will drink a fresh beverage immediately after it is served, it should be the barista's goal to offer every beverage in its ideal form.

There are three steps to serving a milk-based beverage with exceptionally creamy and long-lasting texture.

1. **Steaming.** Steamed milk must have a tight micro-bubble structure. Creating visible bubbles, overheating, and overstretching while steaming can all degrade the potential texture of a beverage.
2. **Pouring.** Pouring with the proper flow and skillfully using "the spoon method" each help delay separation.
3. **Serving.** Present beverages as soon as they are made.

How to Steam Milk

Use the smallest pitcher that can comfortably accommodate the amount of milk needed for the beverage(s) to be made. A good rule of thumb is the pitcher should be about ⅓–½ full before steaming.

1. Puff the steam wand into a moist rag or the drip tray to purge the wand of any condensed water.
2. Set the steam wand tip just below the surface of the milk, near the center. The steam wand should be roughly 10°–30° from vertical.
3. Open the steam wand to full, or nearly full, pressure, depending on the quantity of milk to be steamed. When steaming very small amounts of milk, such as for a macchiato, less pressure is required.
4. Immediately begin the stretching, or frothing, phase and complete it before the milk reaches 100°F (38°C). Once milk is heated above 100°F (38°C), it becomes more difficult to produce quality froth.
5. While stretching, keep the steam tip just below the surface of the milk and carefully aerate the milk without forming any visible bubbles. The aerating should make a consistent, subtle sucking noise.
6. When the desired stretch is achieved, raise the pitcher to sink the steam

wand deeper in the milk. Position the wand so the milk is kept rolling until it *approaches* your desired temperature.

7. Turn off the steam wand, remove the pitcher, wipe the wand with a damp rag, and carefully purge the wand into the rag.

Please note: With some steam wand tips or very high boiler pressure, aerating with the tip at the surface of the milk will quickly lead to over-frothing. In such cases the barista can aerate with the steam tip deeper in the milk, steam with partial pressure, or lower the pressurestat setting.

Milk Textures of Different Beverages

I would like to propose some beverage recipes simply for the sake of this discussion. All beverages presented here will be prepared in classic, Italian-style, 6-oz to 8-oz wide-mouthed ceramic cups, with a base of 1–1½ oz of espresso.

• Cappuccino: Made with very aerated milk. The froth quantity should be such that if the beverage is allowed to fully separate, and then the froth is pushed back with a spoon, the froth will be about ½ inch deep. (This is an estimate and will vary based on the diameter of the mouth of the cup.)

Cappuccino froth should be deep and plush. When it is pushed aside there should be no visible, separate layer of non-aerated milk.

• Café latte: Made with moderately aerated milk. The depth of the froth after separation should be about ¼ inch.

A café latte 2 minutes after it was made. At this point the milk has fully separated.

- Flat white: Made with minimally aerated milk. There should be only a skin of froth on top.

Grooming Milk

No barista will aerate milk perfectly for every drink. If milk is under-aerated, little can be done other than to quickly steam a new pitcher. If the milk is over-aerated, however, the milk can be groomed to achieve the desired texture.

To determine whether milk has been properly aerated, set the pitcher of steamed milk on the counter and *spin* the milk. Spinning consists of moving the pitcher in tight circles without changing its orientation. Spin the pitcher fast enough to whip the milk around the walls of the pitcher in a controlled manner, but slowly enough to prevent bubbles from forming. The more aerated the milk is, the more viscous, or "sticky," it will be when spun.

If it is too aerated, the very frothy top layers of milk should be removed by grooming. To groom, skim the surface of the milk with a large spoon and remove some of the surface froth. Skimming should be done with the bowl of the spoon partially visible, to avoid scooping deeper milk. The surface should be skimmed as evenly as possible. After grooming, spin the milk to evaluate its texture, and if necessary, repeat grooming and spinning. Continue alternating grooming and spinning until the desired milk texture is achieved. The entire grooming process should be completed in no more than a few seconds.

Spinning can also be used to delay milk separation. Effective spinning is rapid enough to keep the surface of the milk glassy but not so rapid that new bubbles form or milk spills.

Coordination of Extraction and Steaming

Milk steaming and espresso extraction should be coordinated so steaming is completed a few seconds before extraction is finished. Espresso is ready to be combined with milk as soon as extraction is completed, but milk requires about 5 seconds to settle after the steam wand is turned off. Any necessary grooming should be done after this short rest.

If extraction is still not complete after the milk has been groomed, the milk should be spun to delay separation. Spinning should not be used as a crutch, however; even when milk is spun, its texture degrades with time, so milk should always be poured within 30 seconds of steaming.

Milk Pouring

I will discuss two milk-pouring methods: free-pouring and the spoon method. Each has advantages and disadvantages, and each has its place in a barista's repertoire.

Free-Pouring

Free-pouring is the dominant system in use today. It involves steaming milk in a spouted pitcher and then simply pouring the textured milk into the espresso. The milk should be poured at a controlled rate slow enough to keep the crema intact but fast enough to prevent the milk from separating in the pitcher. The spouted pitcher is commonly used because it allows the milk flow to be directed, making it easier to create latte art.

Begin by pouring the milk into the center of the crema. Pour quickly enough to prevent separation in the pitcher but slowly enough to keep the crema intact.

Maintain a consistent, moderate flow rate through-out the entire pour. To do this, you must accelerate the tipping motion of the pitcher as the amount of milk in the pitcher decreases.

Rock the pitcher back and forth once the white cloud appears.

Continue rocking the pitcher to create a zigzag pattern. It is critical to resist the urge to raise the pitcher away from the surface of the beverage. It may be counterintuitive, but keep the pitcher as low as possible while pouring and constantly accelerate the tipping of the pitcher to maintain the flow rate.

Back the pitcher toward the edge of the cup while zig-zagging. Once you reach the edge of the cup lift the pitcher a couple of inches and drizzle a small stream of milk back across the cen-terline of the zigzags.

Ecco!

How to Pour Latte Art

To pour latte art you must have a fresh shot of espresso with a reasonable amount of crema and properly textured steamed milk. The milk should look creamy and glassy, with no visible bubbles.

The most common mistakes beginners make are pouring the milk too slowly and lifting the pitcher away from the surface of the beverage while pouring. Pouring milk too slowly can cause it to separate in the pitcher, causing less-aerated milk to pour into the beverage and more-aerated milk to remain in the pitcher. This makes pouring latte art difficult and also results in an under-aerated beverage. Raising the pitcher away from the surface of the beverage causes the milk to dive under the crema rather than resting on top of the crema and forming a design.

> Raising the pitcher while pouring prevents the milk from resting on the crema because the flow of the milk is accelerated by gravity. Raising the pitcher is analogous to diving from a high board: just as the milk dives to the bottom of the cup and hardly disturbs the crema, the diver cuts through the surface of the water with hardly a ripple and submerges deeply. On the other hand, pouring with the spout of the pitcher kept very close to the surface of the beverage is analogous to diving from the edge of a pool: the milk skims the surface of the beverage just as the diver merely skims the surface of the water.

The Spoon Method

The spoon method is common in New Zealand, but I've yet to see it practiced elsewhere. The benefits of the spoon method include delaying froth separation in the cup and allowing control over the texture of the milk while pouring. The disadvantages of the spoon method are it takes more time than free-pouring, requires the use of both hands, and is harder to master.

The spoon method works best with a round bell or vev pitcher with a beveled edge. The wide mouth of the bell pitcher provides a better view of the milk texture while pouring and allows easier spoon access and control.

To execute the spoon method, steam the milk, groom it if necessary, and use a tablespoon as a gate to control the flow and texture of the milk as it is poured. The details are different for each drink, but the basics are the same.

1. Begin the pour with the spoon tightly restricting all but the densest, least frothy milk. Some baristi use the spoon to pull back (away from the pouring edge) the frothiest milk several times before restricting the milk and starting the pour.
2. Pour into the center of the espresso at a moderate rate to prevent breaking up the crema.
3. While pouring, lift the spoon slowly to allow frothier milk into the cup.
4. The surface of the finished drink should be glassy and can be finished with a design if desired.

Pouring a Cappuccino Using the Spoon Method

Begin by tightly restricting the milk flow with a large spoon. Only the least-aerated milk should be allowed into the beverage. Pour at a moderate rate, being careful to keep the crema intact.

Raise the spoon when the cup is one-third to one-half full.

When the cup is nearly full, use the spoon to push very aerated milk onto the surface of the beverage.

Finish the beverage by either drizzling a thin stream of milk back through the centerline of the beverage surface to draw a heart, or by keeping the pitcher where it is to create a white circle framed by dark crema.

Steaming, grooming, and pouring look and feel different when using a bell pitcher; thus, even an experienced barista will need practice and patience to adapt to, and master, using both the bell pitcher and the spoon method.

Spoon Method Variations

Cappuccino. Begin with very aerated, viscous milk. The milk should seem to "stick" to the walls of the pitcher a little when spun. Use the spoon to hold back the lighter surface milk as you pour the densest, least frothy milk into the espresso. When the cup is about ⅓ full, gradually raise the spoon to allow more-aerated milk into the drink. By the time the cup is about ⅔ full, the spoon should be raised completely out of the milk. For the finish, the spoon should be reinserted to push the final bit of very aerated milk into the drink. The surface of the drink should form a crown above the rim of the cup, with a ring of dark espresso framing a round center of glassy white milk.

Café latte. Begin with moderately aerated milk. The milk should be noticeably more viscous than when it was cold, but it should offer almost no resistance to being spun (i.e., it should not stick to the walls of the pitcher.) Use the spoon to hold back the lighter surface milk, and begin the pour. Slowly raise the spoon while pouring to allow more-aerated milk into the drink, and simultaneously raise the pitcher a couple of inches. To complete the drink, lower the pitcher and finish the pour with the spoon either out of the pitcher or restricting just the slightest bit of surface milk. With practice, it is not too difficult to finish the drink with latte art.

Flat white. Begin with minimally aerated milk. The milk should be only slightly more viscous than it was before steaming. Use the spoon to hold back all froth as you pour at a steady pace into the center of the drink, being careful to not break up the crema. Lift the spoon at the final moment to finish the drink with a very thin skin of frothy milk. Traditionally, a flat white's surface is dark with a spot of white in the middle, though some baristi finish their flat whites with a design.

The kiwi who stirred my latte

A few years ago I went to a café in Wellington, New Zealand, and ordered a small latte. The coffee flavor of the first sip was subtler and mellower than that of any latte I'd ever had, and the taste was almost the same on the last sip. Usually lattes start out strong and a bit sharp, since the bulk of the crema is on top, and by the end the drink is milky and weak. Whatever was going on with this drink, it made me want another immediately. This time I watched Dave, the barista, make it for me. First he pulled the shot into the cup and steamed the milk in a spouted pitcher. Then, with a spoon, he restricted the pour tightly to let out an ounce or so of very thin (less-aerated) milk. Next he took the spoon and gently stirred the mixture of espresso and thin milk. Finally, he spun the pitcher briefly and free-poured the rest of the drink. The rosetta on top was gorgeous and the latte tasted as good as the first one.

I chatted with Dave for a long while and learned he always stirred the espresso with a bit of thin milk because he thought it helped distribute the coffee flavor more evenly throughout the drink.

Pour about an ounce of restricted, lightly aerated milk into the espresso and lightly stir.

Why Use the Spoon Method?

I have found drinks made with the spoon method keep their texture intact longer before separating. I'm not sure why this is; possibly by beginning the pour with only the thinnest milk mixing with the espresso, and then gradually increasing the frothiness of the milk introduced, the drink can distribute and "hold" the new froth better. In my experience, if too much frothy milk is introduced too quickly, a drink cannot integrate the new froth, and it ends up sitting on top of the drink instead of mixing in. For instance, try this: begin the pour by pushing the most-aerated milk in first, and then restrict the flow to progressively thinner milk. From the beginning of the pour the frothier milk will not mix well with the espresso, and the drink's texture will never be fully integrated.

Free-Pouring Multiple Beverages from One Pitcher: Milk-Sharing

If a barista were to free-pour a few beverages, one after the other, from one large pitcher, the most-aerated milk would pour into the first drink and each successive drink would have less-aerated milk than the one before. To provide each drink with milk of the desired aeration the barista should "milk-share."

To milk-share, a barista needs to create enough froth in one pitcher for the cumulative needs of all drinks being made. It takes practice to accurately estimate how much to aerate large quantities of milk for multiple beverages. When in doubt, the barista should aim for frothing a little too much, as the excess froth can be removed by grooming.

Once the milk in the large pitcher is steamed, it needs to be "traded" back and forth between the original steaming pitcher and a secondary pitcher. When trading, the topmost, frothiest milk always pours out first. This means the milk in the receiving pitcher initially becomes frothier while the milk in the pitcher being poured from becomes less frothy. A barista should trade until the milk in the original pitcher is of the proper viscosity for the next drink to be poured.

To illustrate milk-sharing with free-pouring, I'll describe how to make one 7-oz cappuccino and one 7-oz café latte.

1. Fill a 20-oz tapered latte art pitcher until the milk is ¼–½ inch below the bottom of the spout.
2. Turn on the grinder.
3. While grinding, empty and wipe clean two portafilters.
4. Purge both groups and reattach one portafilter while preparing the other.
5. Latch the prepared portafilter onto its group. Turn on the grinder. Remove and prepare the second portafilter.
6. Pull both shots simultaneously.
7. Steam the milk so it is about 1½ inches below the rim of the pitcher when steaming is complete.
8. Pour about ⅓ of the milk into an empty 20-oz pitcher.
9. Spin the milk in the original pitcher; it should have the viscosity of cappuccino milk. If it doesn't, trade milk between the pitchers until it does.
10. Pour the cappuccino from the original pitcher; always pour frothier drinks before less frothy drinks.
11. Serve the cappuccino.
12. Pour any residual milk into the second pitcher. The combined milk should be of the right volume and viscosity for the latte. If it is too frothy, groom the milk before pouring. If it is not frothy enough, steam a new pitcher of milk.
13. Pour the latte. Serve.

Pouring Multiple Beverages Using the Spoon Method
When using the spoon method it is not necessary to milk-share. Instead of milk-sharing to manage the frothiness of the milk before pouring each drink, a barista can use a spoon to manage the milk as it pours.

To illustrate how to pour multiple beverages from one pitcher using the spoon method, I'll describe how to make the same two 7-oz beverages, beginning at the point where the shots are in the cups and the milk has been steamed in a 25-oz bell pitcher.

1. Pouring the cappuccino, use the spoon as a gate to initially hold back all froth, and then lift the spoon slowly to allow progressively frothier milk to pour from the pitcher. Compared to making only one cappuccino, the additional froth and milk quantity in the pitcher when pouring multiple drinks requires a more restrictive range of spoon positions, and the barista needs to adapt while pouring.
2. Serve the cappuccino.
3. Spin the pitcher. The remaining milk should be of the proper volume and viscosity for the latte. If it is too frothy, groom the milk or use the spoon to restrict the froth appropriately while pouring the latte.
4. Pour the latte. Serve.

How to Milk-Share

Transfer about ⅓ of the milk from the large pitcher to the small pitcher.

Spin the large pitcher to check the milk texture before pouring.

Free-pour the cappuccino milk using the large pitcher.

Combine remaining milk in the small pitcher.

Spin the milk in the small pitcher. Groom if necessary.

Pour the café latte.

How to Pour Multiple Beverages Using the Spoon Method

Pour a small amount of lightly aerated milk into the café latte, tightly restricting the pour with a spoon. Adding the milk forestalls oxidation of the espresso in the cafe latte.

Pour the cappuccino using the spoon method.

Pour the café latte using the spoon method. It might not be necessary to use the spoon if enough restricted milk was poured in step 1.

With practice, a barista can create latte art using the round pitcher.

An alternative when pouring multiple beverages from one pitcher is to restrict the frothier milk with the spoon, fill each cup about ⅓ full, and then finish the drinks in order from the frothiest to the least frothy. This is an especially useful technique when making more than two drinks at a time.

Pouring up to Four Beverages from One Pitcher
I have seen baristi milk-share to create as many as four beverages from one pitcher (as my friend Jon Lewis did at the 2006 US Barista Championship Finals). With the spoon method it is easy to pour part of the milk for all four drinks and then finish each of the drinks, working from the frothiest to the least frothy.

With free-pouring, however, it is necessary to milk-share and trade milk between two pitchers before pouring each of the first three drinks. If the barista plans well, the milk remaining after the third beverage will be of the proper volume and viscosity for the fourth beverage.

Chapter 5

Barista Systems

Efficiency Enhancement Tools

Busy cafés have little choice but to adopt strategies that are more efficient than simply making one beverage at a time. It is important that baristi are trained to maximize their efficiency without sacrificing quality.

Control Your Grinder with a Programmable Timer

There are numerous benefits to controlling a grinder with a programmable timer. A timer guarantees the consistency of dose sizes, reduces waste, gives a barista the option to attend to other tasks while the grinder runs, and improves the consistency of espresso from shot to shot and barista to barista.

When purchasing a timer I recommend you choose one that is adjustable in increments of tenths of a second or less; infinite adjustability is best. Whatever timer you choose, please first confirm it is compatible with the voltage and amperage of your grinder.

Use Thermometers

Most baristi eschew the use of thermometers, but they shouldn't. The problem with the "touch method" most baristi use is that it is inconsistent from barista to barista, and even an individual barista can be inconsistent over time, especially as the heat sensitivity of his or her fingers decreases with repeated exposure to hot pitchers. The solution is to buy high-quality thermometers, recalibrate them every week, and learn to use them properly. Proper use means the barista must anticipate the temperature reading of the thermometer while steaming. We all know the thermometers measure temperature with a lag, but it is a predictable lag. It is not difficult to learn what the lag is for different quantities of milk, and to simply turn off the steam wand when the thermometer indicates a temperature a certain number of degrees below the target temperature. For example, for 10 oz of milk, turn off the steam 10°F (6°C) early; for 20 oz of milk, turn off the steam 5°F (3°C) early, etc.

It is a mystery to me why so many baristi think they are more accurate than a calibrated thermometer. All baristi should remember the goal is to create a consistent, high-quality product, even if the best technique involves using what some see as a crutch. Just as a concert violinist doesn't rely solely on his or her ear, but uses a tuning fork, a barista should use a thermometer in addition to using his or her senses of touch and hearing to evaluate temperature while steaming. Every café should decide on a standard temperature for its beverages and train baristi to achieve that temperature using thermometers to guarantee consistency.

Baristi who resist the use of thermometers should consider testing themselves by steaming several pitchers with the touch method and then measuring the milk temperatures with a calibrated thermometer. They should also perform this test while multitasking during very busy times to see whether they become less accurate when distracted. If a barista's resulting temperatures vary, perhaps he or she will consider using a thermometer.

To make the use of thermometers less burdensome, baristi can employ a trick I learned from my friend Brant, who owns Small World Coffee in Princeton, New Jersey: Using pliers, bend a small section of the rim of a steaming pitcher in toward the middle of the pitcher. In the bent section, drill a hole just big enough to accommodate the stem of a thermometer. This setup eliminates the need for thermometer clips and holds the thermometer in a convenient spot.

Have a Steaming Platform Available
To some baristi this is sacrilegious, but I think it is acceptable for a barista to hold the milk pitcher in his or her hand during the stretching phase and then set the pitcher on a platform for the remainder of steaming. Alternatively, the pitcher can be set on a platform for the entire stretching and steaming process, though it is more difficult to get perfect results this way.

Hands-free steaming can yield great results, but it takes practice, and it can

Crimp a small area at the rim of the pitcher. In the crimped area drill a hole just large enough to accommodate a thermometer stem.

Barista Systems

The steaming platform should be heavy but easily moved. It should be just tall enough that the tip of the steam wand is about ½ inch above the bottom of the pitcher when the wand is completely vertical.

promote inattention and inconsistency on the part of the barista. When done properly, the result should be no different from the result produced when the barista holds the pitcher.

With some espresso machines the drip tray is positioned well to act as a steaming platform, whereas with other machines it is better to have a heavy, moveable platform that can be easily slid in and out of place below the steam wand.

Workflow

Busy cafés need to implement efficient systems for producing multiple beverages simultaneously. Such systems should be structured but flexible enough to accommodate different numbers of baristi working together. Most importantly, systems should be designed to optimize efficiency without compromising quality.

Efficient Workflow with One Barista

Using the lessons described earlier I would like to outline an efficient system for use when only one barista is working. In this example, one 6-oz cappuccino and two 8-oz café lattes will be made using free-pouring and milk-sharing.

1. Start timer to grind first shot.
2. Fill 32-oz tapered pitcher with milk to ½ inch below bottom of spout.
3. Unlatch and knock out one portafilter, purge group, wipe basket, and dose.
4. As soon as all grounds have been dosed, restart grinder timer.
5. Groom and tamp first portafilter.
6. Attach first portafilter, remove second portafilter, and purge group.
7. Knock out second portafilter, wipe, dose, groom, and tamp.
8. Attach second portafilter, and set one latte cup and one cappuccino cup under portafilters.
9. Start both shots simultaneously.
10. Purge steam wand and begin steaming.
11. Once stretching phase is complete, set pitcher on platform.
12. Restart timer.
13. Unlatch third portafilter, knock out, and wipe.
14. Dose, groom, and tamp third portafilter.
15. As soon as first two shots are complete, stop shots and purge third group.
16. Attach third portafilter, set new latte cup underneath, and start shot.
17. Set first two cups on counter.
18. Turn off steam wand when desired temperature is reached. Wipe and purge steam wand.
19. Pour about ⅓–½ of the milk into a 20-oz secondary pitcher and trade back and forth until milk in secondary pitcher has appropriate viscosity for the cappuccino.
20. Pour cappuccino. Serve immediately.
21. Trade milk between pitchers until both pitchers have milk of equal volume and viscosity.
22. Pour first latte. Serve immediately.
23. Stop third shot when complete.
24. Set third cup on counter.
25. Pour second latte. Serve immediately.

With practice, a skilled barista can get used to simultaneously steaming, grinding, and observing shots. I advise baristi to work as efficiently as they can without sacrificing quality and to attempt to become more efficient over time.

Efficient Workflow with Two Baristi

Busy cafés often require two baristi to work on the espresso machine together. This allows much faster drink production but can lead to coordination problems. As a general rule, one barista should pull shots, and the other should steam milk and finish drinks. The barista on the milk side has the more difficult job and should be the "lead," directing the flow and making decisions. The barista on the espresso side should pull the shots the milk handler calls for and should watch to be sure the right shots end up in the right drinks. If one barista falls behind, he or she should ask the other barista for help so they stay coordinated. For example, if the barista steaming milk is behind by a couple of drinks, he or she should have the other barista steam a pitcher of milk, and possibly finish a drink, in order to prevent any espresso shots from oxidizing. When their tasks are again synchronized, the two baristi can revert to their original roles.

This is the framework of just one possible system. Experienced baristi can, of course, work with a flexible system, but it is a good idea to have a default system to fall back on in case of confusion.

Chapter 6

Drip Coffee

Freshness

Throughout the world drip coffee has a bad reputation, for many good reasons. Many places serve weak, bitter drip coffee after it has sat on a burner or in an air-pot for eternity. Even many "specialty" coffee retailers make the mistake of serving numerous types of coffee simultaneously, thus guaranteeing slow turnover of each coffee and a stale, lukewarm result. It is ironic that a consumer with a $20 machine can make a better and less costly brew at home than he or she might get from a coffee retailer with a $3000 machine. At least at home it's fresh every time.

The simplest thing most cafés can do to improve their drip coffee is to ensure it's always served fresh. Here are some simple ways to serve fresher coffee.

- No matter how busy your café is, do not ever brew more than one variety of coffee at a given time.
- Brew the smallest practical batches such that you are confident you will not run out too frequently.
- Train your employees to brew new batches only when necessary rather than to automatically brew every time a backup urn or airpot is empty.
- If you currently use glass pots or uninsulated metal urns, switch to enclosed, thermal containers.
- Even if you do all of the above, you still need to institute a strict time limit after which coffee must be poured down the drain. In my opinion, serving coffee more than 30 minutes after it was brewed is insulting to a customer who is paying $1.25–$1.75 for a cup. If you don't think it's worth pouring out old coffee, consider how successful a restaurant would be if it regularly served old or stale food. If you still don't think it's worth it, for several weeks drink only coffee that is more than one hour old. If you still don't think it's worth it, you're in the wrong business.
- Train your employees to pour out old coffee rather than be hesitant to "waste" it. It can also be a great selling point to let customers know how much coffee you throw out in order to guarantee freshness.

These freshness standards *will* pay for themselves over time by increasing sales. More sales will, in turn, cause less coffee to go to waste.

Drip Brewing Standards

In the 1950s and 1960s, the Coffee Brewing Institute (later the Coffee Brewing Center) established drip coffee brewing standards still used today. My attempts to find the original Coffee Brewing Center publications failed. The following standards have therefore been derived from the work of the CBC via secondary sources:

DRIP AND FRENCH PRESS COFFEE		
BREWING RATIO	TEMPERATURE	TDS (DRIP ONLY)
3.75 oz grounds to 64 oz water	195°F–205°F (91°C–96°C)	11,500–13,500 ppm

All batches discussed in this chapter are assumed to be brewed using these standards.

Solubles Yield, Brew Strength, and Flavor Profile

The brew strength* of drip coffee is the concentration of solubles in the cup. Brew strength does not indicate flavor quality, but it influences the perception of flavor. If the brew strength of a coffee is too high, it can overwhelm the senses of the coffee drinker and inhibit the perception of subtler flavors.

Solubles yield is the mass of solubles in a brew, expressed as a percentage of the original mass of the coffee grounds used to make the brew. Different solubles dissolve in water at different rates; therefore, each particular solubles yield percentage represents a unique combination of soluble solids and a distinct flavor profile.[26] This can be experienced firsthand by tasting samples from the stream of extract flowing from the brew basket at different points in a brewing cycle.

Coffee made with a lower solubles yield contains a greater proportion of faster-dissolving compounds; these tend to be sour, acidic, bright, and fruity. Higher solubles yields tilt the balance toward slower-dissolving compounds; these generally contribute less acidity and more sweet, bittersweet, and caramel flavors.

Manipulating Solubles Yield and Brew Strength

The relationship between solubles yield and brew strength can be confusing. The following table outlines how to manipulate yield and brew strength by changing the grind and brewing ratio.

Grinding

A relatively uniform grind yields the best drip coffee. Too much particle size variation will result in a combination of overextraction and underextraction throughout the coffee bed.

The best grind setting should always be determined by blind tasting, though a refractometer can be used to measure brew strength and to supplement tasting. If coffee tastes bitter or astringent or feels dry on the tongue, it is overextracted, and

---

* The standard procedure for measuring brew strength directly is to filter the liquid coffee of all insoluble material, evaporate or oven dry the filtered liquid, and then weigh the residual solids. The ratio of the residual solids to the original weight of the (filtered) liquid is the brew strength.

ACTION	EFFECT ON YIELD	EFFECT ON BREW STRENGTH
Make grind finer	Increase	Increase
Decrease brewing ratio	Increase	Decrease
Decrease brewing ratio and make grind finer	Increase	None, if grind is adjusted appropriately
Make grind coarser	Decrease	Decrease
Increase brewing ratio	Decrease	Increase
Increase brewing ratio and make grind coarser	Decrease	None, if grind is adjusted appropriately

the grind is too fine. If coffee is weak or watery, the grind is too coarse. If the coffee tastes both overextracted and weak, it is possible the grinder burrs are dull and need sharpening or changing.

In addition to taste testing, the grind setting can be spot checked visually by observing the wet grounds after a brew cycle is complete. If the beans used were roasted three to seven days before grinding, and ground just before brewing, the majority of the surface of the wet grounds should be covered with froth.

- If there is little or no froth and the grounds are just a little moist (like wet sand), the grind was too coarse.
- If the surface is pitted and/or very muddy, the grind was too fine.

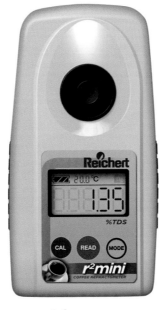

Refractometer

- If there are patches of dry grounds, the grind was too fine, the surface of the coffee bed was too close to the spray head, or some holes in the spray head were obstructed.

Temperature

Brewing water temperature should be between 195°F–205°F (91°C–96°C), depending on roast degree, brewing ratio, and desired flavor profile. A few generalizations can be made about the effects of brewing temperatures on extraction.

- Higher temperatures increase the perception of acidity, bitterness, body, and astringency.[26]
- Higher temperatures generally result in more concentrated extractions, due to the increased solubility of most compounds at higher temperatures. This is true as well for espresso extraction.[21]
- Different temperatures alter the relative solubility of various compounds. This means different temperatures yield not just different cumulative solubles concentrations, but also different relative concentrations of various solubles in the cup.

Turbulence

Turbulence is the chaotic mixing of grounds, gases, and hot water. Turbulence is caused by the release of gases from the grounds when hot water contacts them. Turbulence slows the flow of water through the grounds, delays the wetting of the grounds, and results in the frothy surface seen on wet grounds after brewing.

It is important to have some turbulence because it causes particles to lift and separate, facilitating uniform flow through the coffee bed.[26] In addition, turbulence can improve the evenness of extraction by providing a moving target for the spray head, preventing it from consistently favoring certain patches of grounds. Too much turbulence is a problem because it can excessively delay wetting of the grounds and cause very slow flow rates through the coffee bed, leading to overextraction.

Managing turbulence is not much of an issue if a café consistently brews coffee that is, for instance, four to six days out of the roaster. When the same café has an inventory problem and has to brew coffee roasted either more than ten or fewer than two days ago, it necessary to compensate for the unusual amounts of turbulence.

The beans roasted more than ten days ago create less turbulence and require a finer grind to slow the flow rate. The beans roasted fewer than two days ago will create excessive turbulence. To compensate for too much turbulence a barista has three choices.

1. Use a coarser grind.
2. In the time interval ranging from a few hours before brewing to several minutes before brewing, grind coffee. Many coffee professionals reflexively believe this is a terrible practice, but its effects are comparable to aging coffee a few days longer in whole bean form.

3. If using a programmable brewer, enable the prewet cycle and prewet delay. Prewetting improves the uniformity of wetting throughout the bed and allows some CO_2 to outgas, resulting in more similar flow rates through the bed for all coffees regardless of how long ago they were roasted.

Optimizing Different Batch Sizes

Each combination of machine and brew basket performs best with a limited range of batch sizes, determined by the diameter and shape of the brew basket, the spray head design and flow rate, the size of the drain hole in the bottom of the brew basket, and the permeability of the coffee filter. The most important factor is the brew basket diameter because it determines the height of the coffee bed and hence the appropriate grind setting and contact time. All else being equal, the larger the basket diameter, the larger the optimal batch size.

To achieve a given solubles yield and brew strength when using a machine with a fixed flow rate, a taller bed requires a coarser grind, and a shallower bed requires a finer grind. This is because a taller bed creates more flow resistance and longer *contact (dwell) time* between the grounds and water. Batch sizes outside of the optimum range require excessively fine or coarse grind settings to produce the desired brew strength. Such grind settings can cause the contact time to be too long or short, compromising flavor.

When using a more sophisticated machine with variable spray head flow rates, the same grind can be used for a wide range of bed heights to achieve a given solubles yield and brew strength. With such a machine smaller batches require slower spray head flow rates and larger batches require faster flow rates. The flow rate

Both baskets are designed to fit the same machine. The basket on the right is tapered to accommodate smaller batches.

should be set to result in a constant contact time for all batch sizes. For example, if a half-gallon batch using a particular grind requires a 4:00 brew time, a one-gallon batch may call for a 3:30 brew time.

There is no universal ideal bed height, but the Coffee Brewing Center recommended bed heights of 1 to 2 inches.

How to Brew Very Small Batches
To brew very small batches it is best to use a smaller, tapered brew basket or a wire brew basket insert. Both options decrease the average diameter of the basket interior and increase bed height, allowing a coarser grind to be used than would otherwise be possible with a very small batch.

How to Brew Very Large Batches
To properly brew a large batch with a very tall coffee bed requires opening the *bypass valve*. The bypass reroutes a portion of the brewing water around the filter, diluting the brew without passing the water through the grounds. Using the bypass is the equivalent of using a very high brewing ratio to produce a normal solubles yield and very high brew strength, and then adding water to the pot to decrease the brew strength. In plain English, it dilutes very strong coffee with hot water.

If a batch has a very tall coffee bed and is brewed without the bypass, an excep-

Here is one possible method to determine the proper bypass percentage for a particular grind setting and (large) batch size:
1. Write down the parameters (grind setting, brewing ratio, batch size, and brew strength) that made your coffee taste best in the past with a moderate batch size.
2. Select the new, larger batch size to be made using the bypass.
3. Calculate how much larger the new batch is than the moderate batch. For example, a 1.4-gallon batch is 40% larger than a 1-gallon batch.
4. As an initial guess, set the bypass percentage at half of the percentage from step 3. Continuing the example, the 1.4-gallon batch should be brewed with a bypass of 20%.
5. Brew the new batch, taste it, and measure the TDS. If the TDS (brew strength) is too high, increase the bypass percentage. If the brew strength is too low, decrease the bypass percentage.
6. Continue brewing batches and adjusting the bypass setting until the desired brew strength is achieved.
7. Once you have a successful batch, record the batch size, brewing ratio, grind setting, bypass setting, and brew strength.
8. For the really ambitious coffee geek with a lot of spare time, repeat this process for several batch sizes, all made with the same grind setting. Make a chart with batch size on the *x* axis and bypass percentage on the *y* axis. Plot the successful batches on the chart, connect the dots with a line, and label it "grind setting *z*." Use this chart as a reference tool to determine the bypass setting for any large batch size desired in the future.
9. Frame the chart and give a copy to your mom.

tionally coarse grind is required to limit contact time and prevent overextraction. Attempting to use a very coarse grind to compensate for a very tall bed can create several problems.

- It alters flavor profile.
- It makes extraction a little less uniform because very coarse grinding creates less particle size uniformity.[29]
- In some cases there will be no grind setting both fine enough to provide the necessary brew strength and coarse enough to prevent overflowing from the basket.

The Bypass Valve

For about twelve years I refused to use the bypass because I didn't believe its use could result in great coffee. Then one day my friend Tony, who owns Metropolis Coffee in Chicago, called and said he had had a great coffee at a shop in Michigan that used a 50% bypass! At that point I realized I needed to learn how to use the bypass valve.

The bypass works because it allows the use of a finer grind than would otherwise be possible with a tall bed height. Without the bypass, using a "normal" grind with a tall bed would lead to overextraction, very high solubles yield and very, very high brew strength. When the bypass is used, less water passes through the same tall bed, preventing overextraction and allowing the use of an appropriate grind setting.

How to Determine the Bypass Setting

Experimentation is needed to determine the right combination of bypass percentage and grind setting for a given batch size. One method is to begin with a grind setting known to have produced great coffee in your machine with a moderate batch size and no bypass. The bypass percentage can then be estimated based on how much larger the new large batch is than the previously successful moderate batch. Because grind setting and flavor profile are intimately related, a given grind setting should be able to produce identical flavor profile and brew strength for both "normal" batches and larger batches using the bypass.

A good starting point is to use a bypass setting that is ⅓ the percentage increase in batch size from the 'normal' batch to the bypassed batch. For example, if a normal batch is one gallon and the new batch is 1.5 gallons, the new batch is 50% larger than the standard batch. One third of 50% is 17%, which should be very close to the proper bypass percentage.

Once this initial bypass value is calculated, brew a batch using bypass and the same grind as is used for the standard batch, taste it, and measure the TDS. If the TDS is low, decrease the bypass percentage. If the TDS is high, increase the bypass. If the TDS of both batches is the same, they should taste identical.

Setting Up the Filter

Paper filters are susceptible to absorbing odors during storage[26] and can impart foreign flavors to coffee. To minimize the filter's potential flavor contribution to a brew, the brew basket and paper filter should always be flushed with hot water before use. A flush also rinses any grounds or residue from the brew basket and coffee pot and preheats the basket and pot.

To flush, put an empty filter in the brew basket, slide the basket onto the machine, and brew hot water through the filter and into the empty pot or an urn with

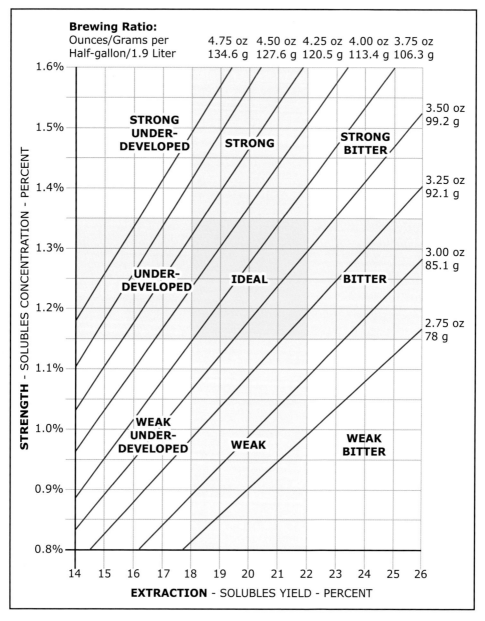

There is a known relationship between brew strength, solubles yield, and brewing ratio; if the values of any two of these variables are known, the third can be calculated.[26] This relationship is illustrated by this ingenious chart published by the Coffee Brewing Center in the 1960s. Reprinted with permission of the Specialty Coffee Association of America, all rights reserved.

Drip Coffee

the tap open. Shut off the water flow after a few seconds. In the case of brewing into a pot or airpot, pour out the water once it has finished flowing into the pot.

After rinsing the filter, load it with grounds and shake the basket back and forth until the surface of the grounds is as level as possible. Be careful not to slide the brew basket onto the machine too forcefully because this can shift the bed of grounds.

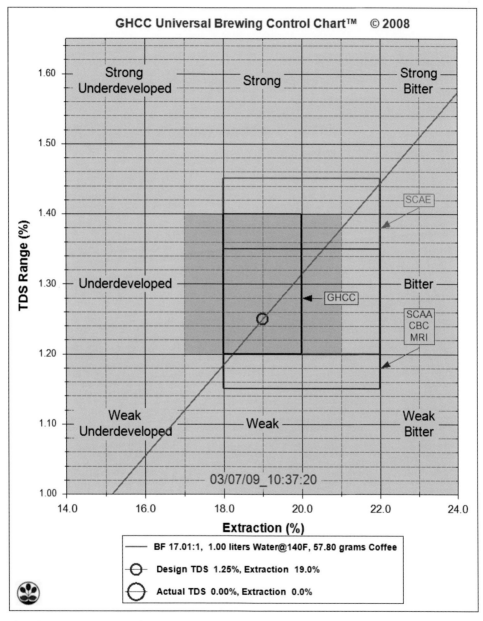

This chart is the creation of Vince Fedele, inventor of ExtractMojo. Vince improved on the CBC chart by correcting the brew formula to reflect the variation in water density as a function of temperature, and by expressing the brew formula as a ratio of water mass to coffee mass, allowing any set of units to be applied to a single, universal brewing control chart.

Stirring to Improve Evenness of Extraction

Stirring can improve extraction when using an open-top brewer or any manual pourover method. Ideally the coffee should be stirred as soon as 5–10% of the water is poured on the grounds. This stir improves the evenness of extraction by ensuring all the grounds are wetted simultaneously.

The barista should stir again as soon as the last of the brewing water has been dispensed onto the grounds. This second stir pulls grounds away from the wall of the filter, preventing grounds from sticking "high and dry" on the filter. If some grounds stick to the upper wall of the filter and cease extracting while grounds at the bottom of the filter continue to extract, the "high and dry" grounds will extract less than the grounds at the bottom of the filter.

I recommend all stirring be done gently, with the minimal necessary agitation of the coffee bed. Aggressive stirring is hard to replicate and may unpredictably accelerate extraction. All else being equal, the more a coffee bed is stirred, the coarser the grind needs to be to achieve a given extraction.

Programmable Brewer Settings

Sometimes I miss the days when temperature and brewing volume were the only drip brewer settings I worried about. Now a barista has programmable control of prewet percentage, prewet delay, bypass percentage, brewing time, and of course, temperature and brewing volume. Having so many options is a bit of a mixed blessing, since I don't think anyone completely understands how they all interact. The manufacturers I've contacted have lamely, if wisely, chosen to offer no programming guidance.

The following is a basic roadmap to programming your machine. Please do not get too hung up on all of these variables; remember that, in the end, taste is the only variable that matters.

Prewet Percentage and Prewet Delay
Prewetting helps improve the uniformity of extraction by wetting and warming the entire coffee bed before extraction begins. This eliminates some of the discrepancy in the extraction rates of the upper and lower layers of the coffee bed. Prewetting is said to help reduce channeling, but that is questionable with most drip brewers.

To set the prewet percentage, experiment to find the largest prewet quantity that does not cause any coffee to flow from the brew basket for 30 seconds after the prewet cycle is complete. Once you have found this setting, start a brew cycle and turn the machine off as soon as prewetting is complete; wait 20–30 seconds, slowly and carefully remove the brew basket, set it on the counter, and use a spoon to excavate the grounds layer by layer. The bed of grounds should be moist throughout. If the lower layers of the bed are dry, a larger prewet percentage is needed. If there are channels of dryness or uneven wetting, it is probably best to not use the prewet option on that machine.

A *prewet delay* is necessary to separate the prewetting phase from the rest of the brewing cycle. A longer delay can be used to drive off more CO_2 and decrease turbulence if the coffee being used is too fresh. When using an exceptionally long delay, it might be necessary to choose a slightly finer grind and to increase brewing temperature by a couple of degrees.

Brewing Time
Brewing time refers to the amount of time it takes to dispense all of the water for a brewing cycle; it has a relatively minor influence on coffee flavor. Brewing time should be adjusted so that a consistent, small pool of water remains on top of the coffee bed during brewing. A very short or very long brewing time might necessitate a change of grind setting.

Bypass, Brew Volume, and Temperature
These parameters have been previously discussed in this chapter.

Common Settings
Based on my discussions with owners of quality cafés, the following are typical ranges for programmable settings when using a 1.5-gallon machine.

DRIP SETTINGS		
Volume	1 Gallon	1.5 Gallons
Prewet Percentage	0%–10%	5%–10%
Prewet Delay	30–45 Seconds	30–60 Seconds
Brewing Time	3:30 – 4:00	3:30 – 4:00
Temperature	200°F–205°F (93°C–96°C)	200°F–205°F (93°C–96°C)
Bypass Percentage	0%	20%–25%

How to Hold Brewed Coffee

Coffee should be held in a sealed, thermal container if it is not going to be consumed immediately after brewing.[26] This minimizes the loss of heat and volatile aromatics to the air. Maintain temperatures of 175°F–185°F (79°C–85°C) to minimize the development of sour flavors during holding.[26] No matter what the holding conditions are, flavor deterioration is noticeable within 15–20 minutes of brewing.

Brewing Drip Coffee to Order

Recently there's been a wonderful drip coffee revolution: in many cafés drip is no longer being brewed in large batches and held for an hour or more before being served. Some cafés have switched to serving coffee from frequently brewed 50-oz French presses, others serve coffee brewed to order in the Clover™ machine, and still others use a rack of 1-cup pourover filters and brew each cup to order.

It seems that the popularity of espresso hasn't killed drip coffee but rather has forced drip coffee to improve and compete for attention.

It is unfortunate and frustrating (at least to me) that so many cafés serve "specialty coffee" that is more than 45 minutes old. I sometimes wonder whether cafés are really saving money or losing customers when they sell such old coffee.

Coffee Filter Types

The porosity and material of the filter used in drip brewing have a significant impact on coffee quality. A more porous filter causes a faster flow of liquid through the coffee bed and requires a finer grind to maintain adequate contact time.

Filter porosity also determines the amount of insoluble material that passes into the brewed coffee. Insoluble material increases the body of coffee but can dull acidity and muddle flavor. Therefore, a choice of filter type involves a trade off between body and flavor clarity; a more porous filter creates more body but less flavor clarity.

All filter types come in a variety of porosities, so it is possible that a metal filter may be more or less porous than a cloth filter. However, the following generalizations are usually true:

- Metal filters produce coffee with a great deal of body and poor flavor clarity. Metal filters must be cleaned thoroughly after each use to prevent the buildup of coffee oils.
- Cloth filters produce coffee with a lot of body and moderate flavor clarity. Cloth filters can make beautiful coffee but are very susceptible to deformation as well as absorption of oils and cleaning chemicals. Like metal filters, cloth filters require diligent cleaning.
- Paper filters produce coffee with the least body and most flavor clarity. Because they are disposable they can be the most expensive option in the long run, but they require the least time and effort to maintain.

Freezing Coffee Beans

Last year I was at my mom's house, and in her freezer I found some Kenya AA beans I'd roasted six years prior. Very curious about the condition of the beans after six years of being frozen, I eagerly brewed a pot. It was really good. That's not to say the beans wouldn't have tasted better if they had been used six years earlier, but it does suggest that freezing is a viable storage method. Since then I've become an avid freezer of beans.

Many myths persist regarding the dangers of freezing coffee beans. Do not believe them.

Freezing works as a long-term storage method because oxidation rates are reduced about fifteen-fold and the coffee oil congeals, greatly reducing the movement of volatiles.[7] Additionally, the scant moisture in roasted beans is bound to the matrix polymer, and therefore nonfreezable.[16]

To freeze beans properly, store them in a nonpermeable sealed container, and remove beans from the freezer only when they are to be brewed. Do not ever allow beans to be defrosted and refrozen.

Chapter 7

French Press Coffee

The French press is very low-tech and has been around for over 100 years, yet French press coffee has arguably never been improved upon. Compared to drip brewing and other percolation methods, a French press provides more uniform extraction from the grounds. Properly made French press coffee has more body and less bitterness, astringency, and underdeveloped flavors than drip coffee.

The coarse mesh of the filter screen in a French press allows a large amount of insoluble bean particles and oils into the cup. This gives French press coffee a tremendous amount of body but poor flavor clarity. If you desire the extraction uniformity produced by a French press but prefer more flavor clarity, make coffee in a French press and then pour it through a filter before serving.

Also, if French press coffee is to be held for several minutes before it is served, it is best to pour it into a preheated thermal container, preferably using a filter to prevent any sediment from getting into the container. Sediment increases the bitterness of coffee during holding.

How to Make Great French Press Coffee

1. Boil water in a kettle, or use hot water from a commercial water boiler. Before pouring, the water should be a few degrees hotter than the desired brewing temperature.
2. Weigh the beans on a gram scale. If you are making coffee at home without a gram scale, use one "coffee scoop," or 2 level tablespoons of grounds, per 4 oz of water.
3. Preheat the press with a little hot water. Pour out this water before adding the grounds.
4. Put the grounds into the press.
5. Put the press on a scale, set the scale to ounces or grams, and tare it.* Please note: 1 oz of water at 200°F (93°C) is 28.3 grams.
6. Weigh the press while pouring. Stop when the desired water weight has been poured.

---

* Do not estimate water volume by sight while pouring. Different coffees will create very different amounts of bloom when struck by the hot water.

79

7. If you do not have a scale handy, use slightly hotter water and measure it by volume in a preheated measuring pitcher before pouring.

8. Set a timer. The proper steeping time is determined by the grind setting. Finer grinds require shorter steeping times, while coarser grinds require longer steeping times.

9. After about 15–20 seconds, stir the coffee to deflate the bloom, or frothy layer, on top of the brewing coffee. The stir helps to wet and submerge the grounds trapped in the bloom.

10. Set the lid on the press, and press down the filter until it sits just below the surface of the coffee. This keeps all the grounds submerged.

11. When the timer sounds, plunge the filter and serve immediately. If desired, pour the coffee through a secondary filter.

French Press Steeping Time

When brewing a new coffee in a French press for the first time, I recommend using a default combination of steeping time and grind. I personally begin with a 3½-minute steep and a corresponding grind setting.

If this default formula produces coffee that is too bright or acidic, the next time I brew it I try a 4-minute steep and a coarser grind. On the other hand, if the default settings produce flat or dull coffee, I change the parameters to a 3-minute steep and a finer grind. I make further adjustments as I gain experience with the coffee.

These settings are simply meant as a guide; you might prefer coffee made with radically different grinds and steeping times.

As soon as the water is poured, the bloom will form at the top of the brew.

After 15–20 seconds, stir the bloom to submerge all of the grounds.

Plunge the screen to just below the surface of the liquid to keep all of the grounds submerged during steeping.

French Press Coffee

Chapter 8
Water

Water Chemistry 101

Water chemistry does not get the attention it deserves in the specialty coffee business. Everyone has heard something like "coffee is 98.75% water," but few people realize how much the water chemistry influences the composition of the other 1.25% as well. Your carbon-filtered water might taste good on its own, but it might still make your prized auction lot Kenya taste no better than a Kenya FAQ brewed with great-quality water.

The Basics

It is common knowledge that brewing water should be carbon filtered and have no "off" flavors. But that is only the starting point for quality brewing water. To get the most out of your coffee (or tea or espresso), the water needs to have a neutral *pH* and appropriate levels of *hardness, alkalinity*, and total dissolved solids (TDS).

The following water chemistry terms are relevant to coffee making.

Total Dissolved Solids (TDS): The combined content of all substances smaller than 2 microns in any dimension dispersed in a volume of water. Measured in mg/L or ppm.

Hardness: Primarily a measure of dissolved calcium and magnesium ions, though other minerals can contribute. Measured in mg/L or grains per gallon.

pH: A measure of acidity derived from the concentration of hydrogen ions; 7.0 is neutral.

Acid: A solution with pH lower than 7.0.

Alkaline: A solution with pH greater than 7.0.

Alkalinity: A solution's ability to buffer acids. Measured in mg/L.

The terms and measurement units used to describe water chemistry often seem designed to confuse. For simplicity I have left out numerous alternative units of measurement and will measure TDS, hardness, and alkalinity in mg/L (milligrams per liter, or parts per million).

> A solution can be very alkaline but have low alkalinity, and vice versa. As an analogy, think of alkaline as the solution's location on the political spectrum. Let's say alkaline refers to being on the right, and acid refers to the left; alkaline denotes being conservative, acid denotes liberal. (No political commentary intended!) Alkalinity, on the other hand, is analogous to stubbornness and resistance to becoming more liberal. Of course, one can be at either end of the spectrum (acid or alkaline) and still be resistant (have high alkalinity) or amenable (low alkalinity) to becoming more liberal.

Terminology

The terms alkalinity and alkaline do not refer to the same thing. "Alkaline" refers specifically to a solution with a pH between 7.01 and 14. "Alkalinity" refers specifically to a solution's ability to buffer an acid or, less technically, its resistance to becoming more acidic.

The relationship between hardness and alkalinity also needs clarification. Hardness is derived from calcium, magnesium, and other cations (positively charged ions). Alkalinity is derived from carbonate, bicarbonate, and other anions (negatively charged ions). A compound such as calcium carbonate contributes to both hardness and alkalinity, because it has calcium (hardness) and carbonate (alkalinity). On the other hand, sodium bicarbonate contributes to alkalinity but not hardness. Common water softeners work by replacing the water's calcium with sodium. This decreases hardness but does not affect alkalinity.

Boiler *scale* is caused by the precipitation of calcium carbonate when hard water is heated. Precipitation of scale decreases the hardness and alkalinity of water. Over the long term, scaling can seriously damage your espresso machine. In the short term, scaling can quickly clog small valves and passageways; gicleurs and heat exchanger restrictors are particularly vulnerable.

Espresso machine manufacturers routinely recommend using water softeners to protect espresso machines. A softener will protect your machine but might ruin your espresso. (See "Water Treatment Options" later in this chapter.)

Brewing Water Standards

I recommend the following water standards for brewing coffee, tea, and espresso.

WATER FOR COFFEE, TEA, AND ESPRESSO			
TDS	PH	HARDNESS	ALKALINITY
120–130 ppm (mg/L)	7.0	70-80 mg/L	50 mg/L

Most industry recommendations call for slightly higher levels of hardness and TDS than listed above; using those industry standards yields marginally better coffee, but I cannot recommend them for espresso because they increase the risk of scale formation.

In theory, water with hardness a little greater than 80 mg/L will not create scale at typical espresso brewing water temperatures. In reality, machine temperatures and the hardness yielded by water treatment systems fluctuate, and I'd rather err on the side of caution. Caution is especially important when using gicleurs or heat exchanger restrictors. Small amounts of scale can dramatically alter the performance of these tiny orifices.

Please note: Hardness of 70 mg/L will create scale at typical steam boiler temperatures. The only way to protect the boiler and still have great brewing water is to install two separate lines with water of different hardness levels feeding the espresso machine.

How Water Chemistry Influences Coffee Flavor

To put it simply, the less "stuff" already dissolved in brewing water, the more "stuff" the water will dissolve from the grounds. If TDS levels are too high, water is a weaker solvent and will not extract enough solubles from the grounds. Coffee brewed with very high TDS water will taste dull and cloudy. Very low TDS water can produce coffee with edgy, unrefined flavors and, often, exaggerated brightness.

Hard water does not decrease the potential quality of coffee or espresso; even if the water feeding the coffee machines is very hard, the actual brewing water will not be too hard because much of the hardness precipitates as scale at typical brewing temperatures. Unfortunately, the scale can damage or alter the performance of heat exchangers, flow restrictors, flow meters, valves, heating elements, and pretty much any other part it comes into contact with. Therefore, hard water makes great coffee but will ruin your machines.

Alkaline water or water with high alkalinity can result in dull, chalky, flat coffee. Water with high alkalinity neutralizes coffee acids, resulting in less acidic coffee. If alkalinity is too low, the resulting coffee will be overly bright and acidic.

Acidic water creates bright, imbalanced coffee. Acidic water and water with low alkalinity can also potentially cause corrosion in boilers.

Water Treatment

Kits to measure water chemistry can be obtained from filtration companies and aquarium supply websites. Every café should have its water tested, both out of the tap and filtered, if filtration is being used. Testing can be done with a purchased kit or by sending water samples to a water treatment company. Please note: The chemistry of water out of the tap can change throughout the year; ideally, the chosen treatment system should be adjustable to compensate for seasonal changes.

Water Treatment Options
Depending on your test results, you might want to try some of these options for water treatment:

Carbon filtration. Improves water's taste and odor but has a trivial effect on TDS and hardness. Every café should use a carbon filter preceded by a sediment filter as the first stage of water treatment.

Reverse osmosis. Removes more than 90% of TDS, hardness, and alkalinity. Straight RO water is too pure for espresso, tea, or coffee brewing. RO water should always be blended with mineral-rich carbon-filtered water or used in conjunction with a remineralizer. Reverse osmosis systems are somewhat expensive and waste a lot of water, but they are relatively low maintenance. Water with very high TDS or hardness should be pretreated, or it will quickly plug the RO membranes in high-volume applications.

Ion exchange resins. Numerous types include softeners, dealkalizers, and deionizers.
- *Dealkalizers:* Replace carbonate and bicarbonate with chloride or hydroxyl. This decreases alkalinity without altering hardness or mineral content.
- *Softeners:* Replace calcium ions with sodium ions to decrease hardness. Softeners are commonly used to protect espresso machines from scale buildup. Fully softened hard water is *not* recommended for espresso making[9] because it inhibits particle wetting, leads to long espresso percolation times,[2,12] and requires a coarser grind to increase the flow rate. Sodium bicarbonate produced by softening can also cause particles to bind,[26] causing erratic, uneven percolation. If softening must be done, the softened water should be blended with mineral-rich carbon-filtered water or treated with a remineralizer. Using softened water with hardness of less than 80 mg/L is not recommended.[9]

• *Deionizers and demineralizers:* Produce pure, or nearly pure, ion-free water, using an anion resin exchange bed and a cation bed in series. Like RO water, deionized water for coffee brewing should be blended with mineral-rich carbon filtered water or used in conjunction with a remineralizer.

• *Remineralizers:* Add minerals to water in order to increase some combination of TDS, alkalinity, and hardness.

How to Choose a Water Treatment System

Before deciding how to treat your water it is essential to get it tested. If you are lucky, the water at your café has reasonable levels of hardness, alkalinity, and TDS and needs to be treated with only a sediment filter and carbon filtration. Almost every treatment system should begin with a sediment filter and carbon filtration.

If your water has very high TDS but a reasonable ratio of hardness to alkalinity, then carbon-filtered water can be blended with RO or deionized water. If the ratio is good but the levels are too low, use a remineralizer.

If the ratio of hardness to alkalinity is very imbalanced, your water might require reverse osmosis or a deionizer to strip the water of nearly all its ions and then a remineralizer to reconstitute the water with the desired chemistry.

There are numerous other scenarios and possible solutions. Before choosing a system it is best to seek the advice of an expert who understands the importance of balanced water chemistry and does not have a vested interest in selling you a water treatment system.

Interestingly, I have found the optimal water chemistry for making tea, coffee, or espresso to be nearly or exactly identical. Moreover, teas, especially the more subtle oolongs, whites, and greens, are more sensitive than coffee to water chemistry. Because the content of dissolved solids in tea is much lower than in coffee, the solids contribution of the water is proportionally greater and has an outsized impact on the quality of tea.

Descaling

If your machine has gicleurs or heat exchanger restrictors, inspect those orifices every few months for scale. If you detect any scale you can easily replace the orifices. Scaling or malfunctioning of those orifices can be a useful early warning system and should be heeded as a potential indication that water hardness is too high. For example, low flow rates from a group head might indicate a clogged gicleur.

If your machine has a serious scaling problem, it needs to be taken apart and descaled. Descaling is a bit of a nightmare, involving chipping scale off parts and then soaking those parts in acids. I recommend you either send a scaled-up machine to an experienced company or use it as an excuse to buy that flash new machine you've been coveting.

Chapter 9
Tea

While many baristi have recently become fanatical about careful espresso preparation, most are still in the dark ages about making quality tea. It would be nice to
see a few more cafés treat their tea programs with a fraction of the respect they give
their espresso programs. As they've learned to do with espresso over the last twenty
years, baristi need to do their part to educate their clientele and offer something
special, or their tea program will always be a wasted opportunity.

Basic Tea-Making Guidelines

To get ideal infusions from a high-quality tea, it is necessary to become familiar with the tea's potential by experimenting with doses, water temperatures, and infusion times. It is also necessary to vary these parameters for successive infusions.

This approach might not be practical for most cafés, so I'll offer the following basic guidelines that will work well with the vast majority of teas.

Dose

For all teas, use 1 gram of tea leaves per 3 oz water. Volumetric dosing (i.e., using 1 tsp per cup) is not reliable because different teas can be of greatly varying densities. Fortunately, dosing by weight will decrease waste in most cafés since most baristi tend to use too large a quantity of leaves. To save time during service, I recommend pre-portioning tea leaves into small containers.

Steeping Time

Optimum steeping time is determined by water temperature, the ratio of the dose of tea leaves to water quantity, and leaf size. Assuming a café uses the same dose for all teas and standardizes water temperature according to tea type, leaf size determines the steeping time. Smaller leaves have more specific surface area and therefore require less steeping time. Larger leaves require longer steeping time; large, tightly rolled leaves need the most time to steep. Generally speaking, teas should be steeped until just before a significant amount of astringency begins to extract. Recommended steeping times range from 30 seconds to 4 minutes.

Rinsing

Some tea types require rinsing, as noted below. To rinse leaves, place them directly in the pot or use a coarse mesh strainer, such that any small tea particles can be flushed along with the rinse water. Fill the pot with warm water for about 10 seconds and then discard the rinse water. Gold filters, fine metal mesh filters, and paper tea bags prevent the flushing of small particles and should not be used for these teas.

General Preparation

Leaves should always be steeped in a preheated, enclosed container and be given ample room to fully expand. Tea balls, tea bags, and small strainers that do not allow the leaves to fully expand are not recommended. Teas with a lot of dust or broken leaves due to handling should be briefly rinsed to eliminate small particles.

The number of quality infusions offered by different teas varies and is influenced by the ratio of leaves to water. Higher ratios and shorter steeping times allow a greater number of quality infusions. For instance, when preparing tea in the traditional Chinese "Gong Fu" style, the ratio may be as high as 1 gram of leaves per 1 oz water. With such a ratio the first infusion may take as little as 10–15 seconds and the leaves may yield as many as 8–10 quality infusions.

Preparation by Tea Type

Black

Steeping time should be carefully managed because overextracted black teas quickly become very astringent. Most black teas offer one or two quality infusions and should be steeped at 200°F–210°F (93°C–99°C). Black Darjeeling is one exception and should be steeped at 190°F–200°F (88°C–93°C).

Oolong

Always rinse oolongs before the first infusion. Oolongs can be steeped three to six times. The first steeping is often too bright or unrefined, the second steeping tends to be the most balanced, and thereafter each successive steeping needs a longer infusion time to extract enough flavor and strength. Steep darker oolongs (browner leaves) at 185°F–195°F (85°C–91°C) and lighter oolongs (greener leaves) at 170°F–185°F (77°C–85°C).

Green

A few green teas, especially ones with rolled leaves or a lot of furry-looking "down," benefit from rinsing; experimentation is required. Due to the enormous variety of green teas and processing methods, ideal steeping temperatures can range from 150°F–180°F (66°C–82°C). Most green teas offer one to three quality infusions.

White

The delicate, subtle flavors of quality white teas are easily damaged by excessively hot water. Ideal steeping temperatures are 160°F–170°F (71°C–77°C), and most white teas offer two to four quality infusions. Whites generally do not require rinsing unless they have a lot of down.

Herbal

To prepare herbal infusions for optimal flavor, steep for 1–4 minutes. For the most potent medicinal benefits, steep for at least 10 minutes in an enclosed container. Steep most herbals in boiling, or nearly boiling, water.

Other Teas

Some teas, such as matcha, pu-erh, frost teas, yerba mate, and various aged teas require unique steeping methods and temperatures. These special cases are beyond the scope of this book, and I recommend that baristi research further before preparing them.

Appendix

Standards

This list is meant as a basic reference. Much of it is derived from current industry standards. The tea recommendations are my interpretations of common, but conflicting, international practices.

WATER FOR COFFEE, TEA, AND ESPRESSO			
TDS	PH	HARDNESS	ALKALINITY
120–130 ppm (mg/L)	7.0	70-80 mg/L	50 mg/L

DRIP AND FRENCH PRESS COFFEE		
BREWING RATIO	TEMPERATURE	TDS (DRIP ONLY)
3.75 oz grounds to 64 oz water	195ºF–205ºF (91ºC–96ºC)	11,500–13,500 ppm

ESPRESSO			
BREWING RATIO	EXTRACTION PRESSURE	EXTRACTION TIME	TEMPERATURE
6.5–20 g grounds to ¾–1½ oz (21–42ml) water	8–9 bar	20–35 seconds	185ºF–204ºF (85ºC–96ºC)

TEA			
TYPE	TEMPERATURE	RINSE?	NUMBER OF QUALITY STEEPINGS
Black	200ºF–210ºF (93ºC–99ºC)	No	1–2
Dark oolong	185ºF–195ºF (85ºC–91ºC)	Yes	3–6
Light oolong	170ºF–185ºF (77ºC–85ºC)	Yes	3–6
Green	150ºF–180ºF (66ºC–82ºC)	Maybe	1–3
White	160ºF–170ºF (71ºC–77ºC)	Maybe	2–4
Herbal	212ºF (100ºC)	No	Varies
All teas: brewing ratio 1 gram tea leaves to 3oz (85ml) water; steeping time 30 seconds – 4 minutes			

Temperature Conversions

TEMPERATURE CONVERSIONS	
FAHRENHEIT	CELSIUS
212	100
—	—
204	95.6
203	95.0
202	94.4
201	93.9
200	93.3
199	92.8
198	92.2
197	91.7
196	91.1
195	90.6
194	90.0
193	89.4
192	88.9
191	88.3
190	87.8
189	87.2
188	86.7
187	86.1
186	85.6
185	85.0
184	84.4
183	83.9
182	83.3
181	82.8

References

1. Petracco, M. and Liverani, S. (1993) Espresso coffee brewing dynamics: development of mathematical and computational models. *15th ASIC Colloquium.*

2. Fond, O. (1995) Effect of water and coffee acidity on extraction. Dynamics of coffee bed compaction in espresso type extraction. *16th ASIC Colloquium.*

3. Cappuccio, R. and Liverani, S. (1999) Computer simulation as a tool to model coffee brewing cellular automata for percolation processes. *18th ASIC Colloquium.*

4. Fasano, A. and Talamucci, F. (1999) A comprehensive mathematical model for a multi-species flow through ground coffee. *SIAM Journal of Mathematical Analysis*, 31 (2), 251–273.

5. Misici, L.; Palpacelli, S.; Piergallini, R. and Vitolo, R. (2005) Lattice Boltzmann model for coffee percolation. *Proceedings IMACS.*

6. Schulman, J. (Feb. 2007) Some aspects of espresso extraction. http://users.ameritech.net/jim_schulman/aspects_of_espresso_extraction.htm

7. Sivetz, M. and Desrosier, N.W. (1979) *Coffee Technology.* Avi Pub., Westport, Connecticut.

8. Cammenga, H.K.; Eggers, R.; Hinz, T.; Steer, A. and Waldmann, C. (1997) Extraction in coffee-processing and brewing. *17th ASIC Colloquium.*

9. Petracco, M. (2005) Selected chapters in *Espresso Coffee: the Science of Quality.* Edited by Illy, A. and Viani, R., Elsevier Applied Science, New York, NY.

10. Heiss, R.; Radtke, R. and Robinson, L. (1977) Packaging and marketing of roasted coffee. *8th ASIC Colloquium.*

11. Ephraim, D. (Nov. 2003) Coffee grinding and its impact on brewed coffee quality. *Tea and Coffee Trade Journal.*

12. Rivetti, D.; Navarini, L.; Cappuccio, R.; Abatangelo, A.; Petracco, M. and Suggi-Liverani, F. (2001) Effect of water composition and water treatment on espresso coffee percolation. *19th ASIC Colloquium.*

13. Petracco, M. (1991) Coffee grinding dynamics. *14th ASIC Colloquium.*

14. Anderson, B.; Shimoni, E.; Liardon, R. and Labuza, T. (2003) The diffusion kinetics of CO_2 in fresh roasted and ground coffee. *Journal of Food Engineering.* 59, 71–78.

15. Pittia, P.; Nicoli, M.C. and Sacchetti, G. (2007) Effect of moisture and water activity on textural properties of raw and roasted coffee beans. *Journal of Textural Studies.* 38 (1), 116–134.

16. Mateus, M.L.; Rouvet, M.; Gumy, J.C. and Liardon, R. (2007) Interactions of water with roasted and ground coffee in the wetting process investigated by a combination of physical determinations. *Journal of Agricultural and Food Chemistry.* 55 (8), 2979–2984.

17. Spiro, M. and Chong, Y.Y. (1997) The kinetics and mechanism of caffeine infusion from coffee: the temperature variation of the hindrance factor. *Journal of the Science of Food and Agriculture.* 74, 416–420.

18. Water treatment information was gathered from the following sources; any inaccuracies are mine.
    http://www.howtobrew.com/section3/chapter15-1.html
    http://www.aquapro.com/docs/BASICWATERCHEMISTRY.pdf
    http://www.thekrib.com
    www.remco.com/ro_quest.htm (reverse osmosis Q&A)
    www.resindepot.com
    Personal communications with staff of Cirqua Inc.

19. Clarke, R.J. and Macrae, R. (1987) *Coffee. Volume 2: Technology.* Elsevier Applied Science, New York, NY.

20. Spiro, M.; Toumi, R. and Kandiah, M. (1989) The kinetics and mechanism of caffeine infusion from coffee: the hindrance factor in intra-bean diffusion. *Journal of the Science of Food and Agriculture.* 46 (3), 349–356.

21. Andueza, S.; Maeztu, L.; Pascual, L.; Ibanez, C.; de Pena, M.P. and Concepcion, C. (2003) Influence of extraction temperature on the final quality of espresso coffee. *Journal of the Science of Food and Agriculture.* 83, 240–248.

22. Pittia, P.; Nicoli, M.C. and Sacchetti, G. (2007) Effect of moisture and water activity on textural properties of raw and roasted coffee beans. *Journal of Texture Studies.* 38, 116–134.

24. Labuza, T.P.; Cardelli, C.; Anderson, B. and Shimoni, E. (2001) Physical chemistry of roasted and ground coffee: shelf life improvement for flexible packaging. *19th ASIC Colloquium.*

25. Leake, L. (Nov. 2006) Water activity and food quality. *Food Technology.* 62–67.

26. Lingle, T. (1996) *The Coffee Brewing Handbook.* Specialty Coffee Association of America, Long Beach, CA.

27. Zanoni, B.; Pagharini, E. and Peri, C. (1992) Modelling the aqueous extraction of soluble substances from ground roasted coffee. *Journal of the Science of Food and Agriculture.* 58, 275–279.

28. Spiro, M. (1993) Modelling the aqueous extraction of soluble substances from ground roasted coffee. *Journal of the Science of Food and Agriculture.* 61, 371–373.

29. Smith, A. and Thomas, D. (2003) The infusion of coffee solubles into water: effect of particle size and temperature. *Department of Chemical Engineering,* Loughborough University, UK.

30. Illy, E. (June 2002) The complexity of coffee. *Scientific American.* 86–91.

Glossary

Acidity   The sharpness, snap, sourness, or liveliness of coffee.

Alkaline   A solution with a pH greater than 7.0.

Alkalinity   A solution's ability to buffer acids.

Aroma   A quality that can be detected by the olfactory system.

Bimodal   Having two modes, or values, that occur most frequently.

Body   A beverage's weight or fullness as perceived in the mouth.

Bottomless portafilter   A portafilter with its undercarriage sawed off to allow viewing of the bottom of the basket during extraction.

Brew colloids   Materials smaller than one micron in any dimension that are dispersed in a coffee. Made up of a combination of oils and cell wall fragments.

Brew strength   The concentration of solids (or solubles) in an espresso (or coffee).

Brewing ratio   The ratio of dry grounds to water used to make a coffee.

Bypass valve   A channel used to divert a predetermined proportion of the brewing water around the grounds during drip brewing.

Café crema   A very long pull of espresso.

Channel   An area of high-velocity flow through a coffee bed.

Compact layer   A densely packed solid mass that can form at the bottom of the coffee bed during espresso percolation.

Concentration gradient   The difference in concentration of coffee solids from within the grounds to the surrounding liquid.

Contact time (dwell time)   The amount of time the grounds and brewing water remain in contact.

Crema   Espresso foam composed primarily of CO_2 and water vapor bubbles wrapped in liquid films made up of an aqueous solution of surfactants. Also contains dissolved coffee gases and solids, emulsified oils, and suspended coffee bean cell wall fragments.

Cupping   A standardized procedure for evaluating roasted and ground coffee.

Deadband   The difference between the actuation and deactuation points of a pressure-stat.

Degassing (outgassing)   The release of gases, particularly CO_2, by roasted coffee beans.

Diffusion   The movement of a fluid from an area of higher concentration to an area of lower concentration.

Emulsion   A suspension of small globules of oil in an espresso in which the oil and liquid are immiscible.

Extraction   The removal of mass from coffee grounds.

Espresso brewing ratio   The ratio of the mass of a dry dose of espresso grounds to the mass of the shot produced by the grounds.

Fines   Tiny coffee bean cell wall fragments produced by grinding.

Fines migration   The transport of fines by the brewing liquid as it percolates through a coffee bed.

Finger-strike dosing   A method of grooming a dose of espresso grounds by swiping a straightened finger across the surface of the dose.

Flavor   The combined sensation of a substance's taste and aroma.

Gicleur   A small orifice that limits water flow to the group head in an espresso machine.

Grooming   The leveling and refining of a dose of espresso grounds.

Hardness   A measure of calcium and magnesium ions dissolved in water.

Heat exchanger   A small pipe within an espresso machine boiler where water is flash-heated on its way to the group head.

Infusion   A solution produced by steeping in water.

Insoluble   Cannot dissolve in water.

Lungo   A "long" shot of espresso. When defined by mass and brewing ratio: a shot weighing approximately three times the mass of the dose of dry grounds used to produce it.

Mouthfeel   The in-mouth tactile sensations produced by a beverage.

Normale   A "standard" shot of espresso. When defined by mass and brewing ratio: a shot weighing approximately twice the mass of the dose of dry grounds used to produce it.

Overextraction   The removal of more than the desired amount of mass from the grounds when making a coffee or tea.

Percolation   The passing of water through a porous medium.

pH   A measure of how acid or alkaline a solution is.

PID controller   Proportional integral derivative controller. Installed in an espresso machine to improve brewing water temperature consistency.

Preinfusion   A brief wetting of espresso grounds before full-pressure infusion begins.

Pressure profile   A graphical representation of pressure values relative to time throughout a shot.

Pressurestat   A device in an espresso machine that maintains boiler pressure within a predetermined range by activating and deactivating the heating element.

Prewet delay   An interruption in water flow from the spray head after a prewetting cycle.

Prewetting   In drip brewing, an initial wetting of the grounds followed by a delay before the rest of the brewing water is dispensed by the spray head.

Prosumer   Of professional quality but designed for serious consumers.

Ristretto   A "short" shot of espresso. When defined by mass and brewing ratio: a shot weighing approximately the same amount as the dose of dry grounds used to produce it.

Scale   Deposits of calcium carbonate precipitated from water.

Solids yield   The percentage of mass removed from the grounds during espresso extraction.

Soluble   Can dissolve in water.

Solubles yield   The percentage of mass removed from grounds during drip brewing.

Specific heat   The ratio of the quantity of heat required to raise the temperature of a substance 1° to that required to raise the temperature of an equal mass of water 1°.

Specific surface area   Surface area per unit mass or volume.

Spinning   A technique to delay milk separation in the pitcher after steaming.

Surfactants   Any dissolved substance in a solution that reduces its surface tension.

Taste   The components of flavor perceived by the tongue.

Temperature profile   A graphical representation of temperature values relative to time throughout a shot.

Temperature surfing   A technique used to manipulate temperature on heat-exchange espresso machines.

Thermosyphon loop   A pipe in which water circulates between the heat exchanger and group head of an espresso machine.

Total dissolved solids (TDS)   The combined content of all substances smaller than 2 microns in any dimension dispersed in a volume of water; measured in mg/L or parts per million (ppm).

Trimodal   Having three modes, or values, that occur most frequently.

Turbulence   The chaotic mixing of grounds, gases, and hot water caused by the release of gases from the grounds when contacted by hot water.

Underextraction   The removal of less than the desired amount of mass from the grounds when making a coffee or tea.

Volatile aromatics   Soluble gases that contribute to the aroma of coffee.

Index

About the Author

Scott Rao was bitten by the coffee bug in 1992 when he discovered City Bean Coffee in Los Angeles. Scott had always loved coffeehouses, but until that first cup of Java Blawan from City Bean he had never enjoyed the taste of coffee. That cup changed his life, and Scott immediately decided he wanted to learn everything he could about coffee and open a coffeehouse.

In 1994 Scott founded Rao's Coffee in Amherst, Massachusetts, and sold it in 2001. In 2006 Scott founded Esselon Café in Hadley, Massachusetts. He left Esselon in 2007. During his career Scott has roasted and sampled more than twenty thousand batches of coffee and made several hundred thousand coffee beverages.

Scott currently does consulting for coffee retailers. He no longer has any formal ties to Rao's Coffee or Esselon Café.

Scott can be reached at scott.rao@gmail.com.

Please visit *www.theprofessionalbaristashandbook.com* for information about purchasing this book.